YOUR TAX FORMS
MADE EASY

2001

GRAHAM M. KITCHEN FCA

CONSULTANT EDITOR
BRIAN GILLIGAN FCA, ATII, TEP
OF BDO STOY HAYWARD,
CHARTERED ACCOUNTANTS

foulsham
LONDON • NEW YORK • TORONTO • SYDNEY

foulsham

The Publishing House, Bennetts Close
Cippenham, Slough, Berks SL1 5AP

ISBN 0-572-02600-5

The tax forms reproduced in this book are Crown copyright
and printed with permission of the Inland Revenue. As this
book went to press prior to the new fiscal year, the forms
reproduced are draft versions.

Printed in Great Britain by Bath Press Ltd, Bath.

Contents

Introduction

How to use this book

When you get a tax form, look it up in the contents page of this book to identify it, turn to the appropriate chapter and that will tell you what you need to do with the form. If the form needs to be filled in, this book will tell you how to do this, where to get the information – plus a few tax tips along the way! There is a summary of rates and allowances, including those announced in the March 2001 Budget, on page 69.

Tax return form

Not everyone gets a tax return automatically. They are normally sent out to people who have more than one source of income or are higher-rate tax payers; to all company directors; to the self-employed and to anyone whose tax affairs are fairly complex.

The fact that you do not get a tax return doesn't mean that you don't have to complete one.

The responsibility is yours – not your employer's, nor the tax office's. If you have received earnings or income which hasn't been taxed, or you think you have paid too much tax and you are entitled to a tax refund, then you should fill in a tax return.

You have the opportunity to work out, on tax calculation forms, your own tax liability or tax refund if you so wish (see pages 63–4).

You can submit your tax return electronically via the internet on **www.ir-efile.gov.uk/**

Where do you get a form?

If you want a tax return form contact your local tax office; if you want the supplementary pages, telephone the special Inland Revenue order line on 0845 9000 404. You will need to quote your name, address and NI reference number. You can also request forms and notes in large print, audio or in Braille format by contacting your local tax office. The Inland Revenue have a helpline which you can ring on 0845 9000 444. There is also a website – **www.inlandrevenue.gov.uk/sa** from which you can download forms, or you can order by e-mail on **saorderline.ir@gtnet.gov.uk**

When should you fill in a tax return?

Unfortunately, the tax year does not follow the calendar year – it runs from 6 April to 5 April – just to confuse everyone!

The 2001 tax return covers your income, capital gains, reliefs and allowances for the year ended 5 April 2001.

Although it is called a self assessment tax return you do not have to calculate your own tax if you don't want to. Provided that you send in your tax return by 30 September 2001 (or two months after the date the tax return was sent to you, if later), the tax office will do it for you.

If you wish to use the tax calculator working sheets provided with your tax return, then you have until 31 January 2002 to send in your return (see page 62).

Payments on account

If you have not paid most of your tax by deduction, or you are self-employed, you should have paid an amount on account of your 2000–2001 tax liability on 31 January 2001 (see page 29).

Don't be late

There will be an automatic penalty of £100 if your tax return is not sent in by 31 January 2002 and another £100 six months later if it is still overdue. (These are reduced if the tax due is less than £100.)

There will be further penalties if you continue to be late. In addition, interest and surcharges will be charged on overdue tax.

Do you have to fill in a tax return if you are *always* due a refund?

No; the tax office will probably send you a form R40 which is a simplified form of return and which should result in your tax refund coming through regularly and quickly (see page 54).

Go back six years

If you find you have been paying too much tax this year, there is a good chance that this has happened in previous years. You can go back six years to reclaim tax.

Are you claiming tax refunds due to you?

The Inland Revenue estimates that around seven million pensioners, married women and children are not claiming their tax refunds.

If your total income does not exceed your tax allowances and you have received any income from which tax has been deducted, you should claim it back. Turn to page 54 for advice on what to do or telephone the taxback helpline on 0845 077 6543.

If you are on PAYE

Don't assume that your PAYE code is correct. Your employer cannot check it for you – you must do it yourself (see page 52); it's also up to you to check that the tax that you have paid during the year is correct (see page 62).

What to do if you don't get a reply from your tax office

Under the Taxpayer's Charter you should not have to wait more than eight weeks for a reply to your query. Contact your local tax enquiry office if you have a query, then your tax inspector.

If you still do not get satisfaction, write to the director of your regional tax office and as a last resort to the Adjudicator's Office at 28 Haymarket, London SW1Y 4SP – all telephone numbers are in the telephone directory under Inland Revenue. You will find more information in Inland Revenue leaflet IR120.

How this book can help you

Each page corresponds to a section of your tax return or tax form, and you are told what to enter, what *not* to enter and where to find the information that the tax office needs.

There are many tax tips and additional chapters to give you extra advice in claiming tax back and checking your own tax.

Why this book is useful to you

1. It will make it easier for you to fill in your tax return.
2. It will tell you whether you are due a tax refund and, more importantly, how to claim it.
3. You will avoid paying too much tax because you can identify the form you have received and know what to do with it.
4. You can fill in the tax return form reproduced in this book so that you have a permanent copy to which you can refer at any time.
5. It will give you a better understanding as to how the tax system works so you can use it to your best advantage.

How to fill in your tax return

Start filling in your new self assessment tax return by ticking either the 'No' or 'Yes' boxes (Q1 to Q9) on page 2 of the return (reproduced below).

If you tick 'Yes' in any box, check to see if the tax office have sent you the supplementary pages to complete and tick them off in the right hand column.

You will need supplementary pages if you are:

Reference number		Page in this book
SA101	In employment	31
SA102	Participating in share schemes	35
SA103	Self-employed	36
SA104	In partnership	42
SA105	Owning land or property	44
SA106	Receiving foreign income	47
SA107	Receiving income from trusts or estates	48
SA108	Declaring capital gains or losses	49
SA109	Non-resident in the UK	51

If you need supplementary pages and you have not been sent them with your tax return, ring the Inland Revenue order line on 0845 9000 404 (fax 0845 9000 604) and ask for the missing pages. These forms can also be downloaded from the website **inlandrevenue.gov.uk/sa** You will need to quote your name, address and NI reference number.

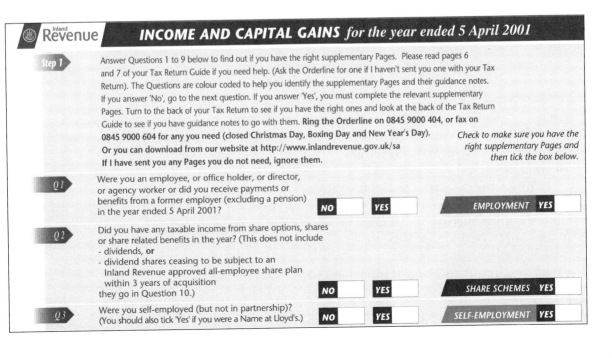

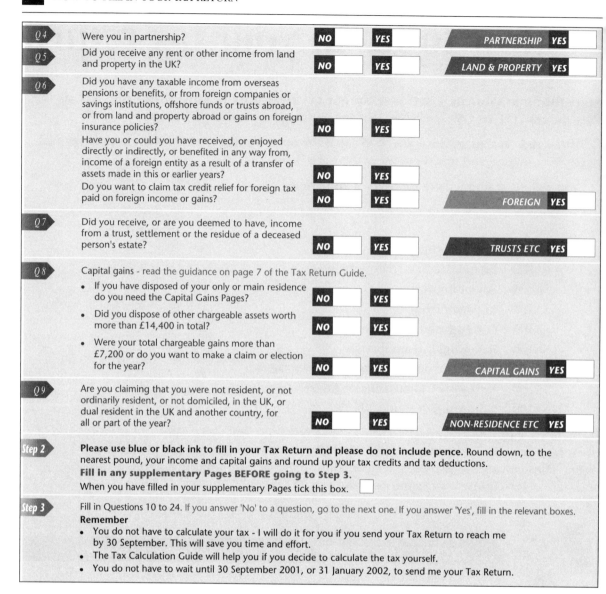

Q4 Were you in partnership? NO [ ] YES [ ] PARTNERSHIP YES [ ]

Q5 Did you receive any rent or other income from land and property in the UK? NO [ ] YES [ ] LAND & PROPERTY YES [ ]

Q6 Did you have any taxable income from overseas pensions or benefits, or from foreign companies or savings institutions, offshore funds or trusts abroad, or from land and property abroad or gains on foreign insurance policies? NO [ ] YES [ ]

Have you or could you have received, or enjoyed directly or indirectly, or benefited in any way from, income of a foreign entity as a result of a transfer of assets made in this or earlier years? NO [ ] YES [ ]

Do you want to claim tax credit relief for foreign tax paid on foreign income or gains? NO [ ] YES [ ] FOREIGN YES [ ]

Q7 Did you receive, or are you deemed to have, income from a trust, settlement or the residue of a deceased person's estate? NO [ ] YES [ ] TRUSTS ETC YES [ ]

Q8 Capital gains - read the guidance on page 7 of the Tax Return Guide.
- If you have disposed of your only or main residence do you need the Capital Gains Pages? NO [ ] YES [ ]
- Did you dispose of other chargeable assets worth more than £14,400 in total? NO [ ] YES [ ]
- Were your total chargeable gains more than £7,200 or do you want to make a claim or election for the year? NO [ ] YES [ ] CAPITAL GAINS YES [ ]

Q9 Are you claiming that you were not resident, or not ordinarily resident, or not domiciled, in the UK, or dual resident in the UK and another country, for all or part of the year? NO [ ] YES [ ] NON-RESIDENCE ETC YES [ ]

Step 2 **Please use blue or black ink to fill in your Tax Return and please do not include pence.** Round down, to the nearest pound, your income and capital gains and round up your tax credits and tax deductions.
Fill in any supplementary Pages BEFORE going to Step 3.
When you have filled in your supplementary Pages tick this box. [ ]

Step 3 Fill in Questions 10 to 24. If you answer 'No' to a question, go to the next one. If you answer 'Yes', fill in the relevant boxes.
Remember
- You do not have to calculate your tax - I will do it for you if you send your Tax Return to reach me by 30 September. This will save you time and effort.
- The Tax Calculation Guide will help you if you decide to calculate the tax yourself.
- You do not have to wait until 30 September 2001, or 31 January 2002, to send me your Tax Return.

The next step

If you have ticked any of the 'Yes' boxes above, then the next step is to fill in those supplementary pages – turn to the appropriate page reference in this book before you go on to complete the rest of the tax return.

If you have ticked all the 'No' boxes, then start to fill in page 3 of your tax return, which covers income from UK savings and investments.

The tax return is reproduced on the following pages.

There is a 'Fill this in if …' box after each section so that you can identify quickly whether it applies to you or not. If it does, there are boxes telling you where to find the information, and what to enter.

There are lots of tax tips and reminder boxes along the way.

Q10 Income from UK savings and investments

If you receive income from UK savings and investments tick the 'Yes' box and fill in the information requested. If you tick the 'No' box, turn to Q11 on page 12.

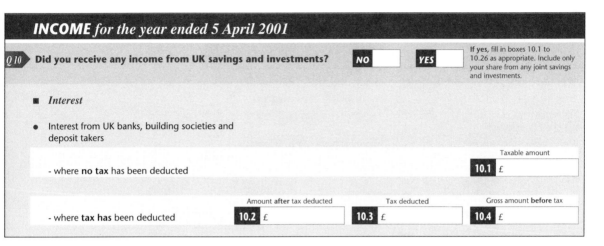

INCOME *for the year ended 5 April 2001*

Q 10 ▶ **Did you receive any income from UK savings and investments?**   NO [ ]   YES [ ]

If yes, fill in boxes 10.1 to 10.26 as appropriate. Include only your share from any joint savings and investments.

■ *Interest*

● Interest from UK banks, building societies and deposit takers

- where **no tax** has been deducted

Taxable amount
10.1 £

	Amount **after** tax deducted	Tax deducted	Gross amount **before** tax
- where **tax has** been deducted	**10.2** £	**10.3** £	**10.4** £

FILL THIS IN IF:

You have savings accounts with banks, building societies and other deposit takers in the UK.

TAX TIP:

If you have savings or investments held in joint names, the interest is normally divided equally when filling in tax returns. If the ownership is not held equally, then you should ask the tax office for form 17 in which you can jointly declare the actual ownership split. You then enter the amounts accordingly in your tax returns. Such declaration takes effect from the date it is made, provided that the form is sent to the tax office within 60 days.

WHERE TO FIND THE INFORMATION

Your bank, building society, etc. should send you an annual statement showing the interest earned and any tax deducted. If you do not receive a statement, ask for one.

TAX TIP:

Did you receive your interest gross or net of tax?
If you did not instruct your bank or building society to pay your interest gross by filling in form R85, then they will deduct tax. If your total income in 2001–2002 is likely to be less than £4,535 you should ask your bank or building society for form R85 otherwise you will have to reclaim the tax at the end of the year (see page 54).

What to enter

You do not need to state the name of the bank, building society, etc.

Where no tax has been deducted, fill in box 10.1 with the *total* amount you received in the year ended 5 April 2001.

Where tax *has* been deducted, fill in boxes 10.2, 10.3 and 10.4 with the totals.

You will need to keep a note of how you arrive at the total – use the tax organiser on page 72 of this book.

	Amount after tax deducted	Tax deducted	Gross amount before tax
• Interest distributions from UK authorised unit trusts and open-ended investment companies (dividend distributions go below)	**10.5** £	**10.6** £	**10.7** £

FILL THIS IN IF:	WHERE TO FIND THE INFORMATION
You have interest from UK unit trusts, etc.	Your unit trust, etc. will provide you with a tax voucher.

What to enter

The total gross amount, total tax deducted and total after tax.

If you received interest without tax being deducted, include the figure in 10.7, with a zero value in your total for box 10.6.

Do not include any 'equalisation' receipts.

Include any interest reinvested in accumulation units in shares.

			Taxable amount
• National Savings (other than FIRST Option Bonds and Fixed Rate Savings Bonds and the first £70 of interest from a National Savings Ordinary Account)			**10.8** £

	Amount after tax deducted	Tax deducted	Gross amount before tax
• National Savings FIRST Option and Fixed Rate Savings Bonds	**10.9** £	**10.10** £	**10.11** £

FILL THIS IN IF:	WHERE TO FIND THE INFORMATION	What to enter
You have any interest from a National Savings ordinary account (apart from the first £70) or investment accounts, deposit, income or capital bonds, Pensioners' Guaranteed Income Bonds, FIRST Option Bonds or Fixed Rate Savings Bonds.	If you receive interest from a National Savings ordinary account, send your book to National Savings, Glasgow, G58 1SB to have the interest added. Show the total interest in your tax return but exclude the first £70 of interest as it is tax free. Interest is credited automatically on your investment account every 31 December and a statement will be sent to you if you request one. The tax office will accept this December interest figure as the figure to go in your tax return; you do not have to apportion it on a time basis. National Savings will send you an annual statement of interest earned on bonds in April each year.	The total interest received or credited in your accounts in the year ended 5 April 2001 in respect of the National Savings accounts and bonds goes in box 10.8. Interest from FIRST Option Bonds will have had tax deducted so fill in the boxes 10.9, 10.10 and 10.11 for these.

DO NOT FILL THIS IN IF:

You only have interest from any National Savings Certificates or Children's Bonus Bonds – these do not have to be declared in your tax return. Neither do you need to give details of any Premium Bond or Lottery winnings.

	Amount after tax deducted	Tax deducted	Gross amount before tax
• Other income from UK savings and investments (except dividends)	**10.12** £	**10.13** £	**10.14** £

FILL THIS IN IF:

You have any income from UK savings, etc. not covered in the earlier sections. These could include, for example, purchased annuities (but not those arising from a personal pension or retirement contract); income from Government stocks; friendly societies. This section could also be used for profits on relevant discounted securities and profits on selling certificates of deposit, etc.

WHERE TO FIND THE INFORMATION

Annuity statements and other documentation, certificates and interest vouchers from investment and insurance companies.

TAX TIP:

If most of your income comes from interest you may be due a tax refund – see page 54.

What to enter

The total amount received, tax credit or tax deducted and gross income.

If you have accrued income reliefs exceeding charges, the net figure should be deducted from box 10.14 without any adjustment to box 10.13.

Do not include any dividends – this section is for interest only.

■ *Dividends*

	Dividend/distribution	Tax credit	Dividend/distribution plus credit
• Dividends and other qualifying distributions from UK companies	**10.15** £	**10.16** £	**10.17** £

	Dividend/distribution	Tax credit	Dividend/distribution plus credit
• Dividend distributions from UK authorised unit trusts and open-ended investment companies	**10.18** £	**10.19** £	**10.20** £

	Dividend	Notional tax	Dividend plus notional tax
• Scrip dividends from UK companies	**10.21** £	**10.22** £	**10.23** £

		Notional tax	Taxable amount
• Non-qualifying distributions and loans written off	**10.24** £	**10.25** £	**10.26** £

What to enter

Put in each of the boxes the total amounts you received, the tax credit (or notional income tax) and the gross amount (the dividend received plus the tax credit). Include scrip and stock dividends but do not include 'equalisation' receipts.

FILL THIS IN IF:

You received dividends or distributions from UK companies.

WHERE TO FIND THE INFORMATION

The dividend vouchers and distribution receipts will show all these details.

REMEMBER:

If you pay tax at the starting or basic rate, the tax credit (10%) meets your tax bill on this income. If you are a higher-rate taxpayer the tax credit is treated as a payment on account of any tax due. If, however, you are a non-taxpayer you cannot reclaim this tax credit.

Q11 Income from a UK pension, retirement annuity or Social Security benefit

If you received income from a UK pension, retirement annuity or Social Security benefit, tick the 'Yes' box and fill in the information requested. If you tick the 'No' box, turn to Q12 on page 14.

INCOME *for the year ended 5 April 2001, continued*

11 Did you receive a taxable UK pension, retirement annuity or Social Security benefit? *Read the notes on pages 12 to 14 of the Tax Return Guide.*	NO ☐ YES ☐	If yes, fill in boxes 11.1 to 11.13 as appropriate.

■ **State pensions and benefits**

Taxable amount for 2000-2001

● State Retirement Pension *(enter the **total** of your entitlements for the year)* — **11.1** £

● Widow's Pension — **11.2** £

● Widowed Mother's Allowance — **11.3** £

FILL THIS IN IF:	**WHERE TO FIND THE INFORMATION**
You were entitled to a State pension, widow's pension or widowed mother's allowance between 6 April 2000 and 5 April 2001.	You should have a statement from the Department of Social Security of the pensions and allowances to which you are entitled – if not, ask at your local office.

What to enter

Any basic State pension including any earnings-related pension, graduated pension and age addition. A married man should only enter amounts payable to him; a married woman should enter amounts payable to her in *her* tax return (even if paid as a result of her husband's contributions), including any widow's pension or widowed mother's allowance. Include any earnings related increase with the widowed mother's allowance but exclude any child dependency increase.

Do not enter

The State Christmas bonus, winter fuel payment or other social security benefits in this section.

TAX TIP:
If the State pension is going to be your only income, then you can, and should, apply to your local Social Security Office for income support, housing benefit and various other social security benefits which are not taxable and need not be included in your tax return. Also apply to your local council for a reduction in your council tax.

● Industrial Death Benefit Pension		**11.4** £	
● Jobseeker's Allowance		**11.5** £	
● Invalid Care Allowance		**11.6** £	
● Statutory Sick Pay and Statutory Maternity Pay paid by the Department of Social Security		**11.7** £	
	Tax deducted	Gross amount before tax	
● Taxable Incapacity Benefit	**11.8** £	**11.9** £	

FILL THIS IN IF:

You received or were entitled to any of the following benefits in the year ended 5 April 2001: Industrial death benefit, statutory sick pay and maternity pay paid by the DSS, jobseeker's allowance, taxable incapacity benefit, invalid care allowance.

WHERE TO FIND THE INFORMATION

Your benefit office will have given you a statement or form showing the amount payable and, where applicable, the taxable portion of the benefit.

TAX TIP:

If you receive a pension in addition to the State pension it is possible you may be able to claim some tax back (see page 54).

What to enter

State the taxable amount received or due to you for the year ended 5 April 2001 in the relevant box.

In the case of incapacity benefit the DSS will give you a form advising of the tax position. (It is not taxable for the first 28 weeks of incapacity or if paid when incapacity began before 13 April 1995 and for which invalidity benefit used to be payable.)

Statutory sick pay or statutory maternity pay should only be shown if paid direct to you by the DSS; if it was paid to you by your employer then it will be included on your P60 or P45 form.

■ *Other pensions and retirement annuities*			
	Amount after tax deducted	Tax deducted	Gross amount before tax
● Pensions (other than State pensions) and retirement annuities	**11.10** £	**11.11** £	**11.12** £
	Amount of deduction		
● Deduction *- see the note for box 11.13 on page 14 of your Tax Return Guide*	**11.13** £		

FILL THIS IN IF:

You received a pension other than the State pension between 6 April 2000 and 5 April 2001.

WHERE TO FIND THE INFORMATION

At the end of each tax year the company paying you the pension must send you a P60 form (see page 56) or a statement by 31 May 2001.

What to enter

The gross amount received, the tax deducted and the amount actually received in the year ended 5 April 2001.

Certain pensions are exempted in whole or part from UK tax, in which case enter the amount in box 11.13.

Q12 Other income you may have received

This section covers less familiar forms of income which will not apply to the majority of taxpayers. If you have received any of these, tick the 'Yes' box and fill in the information requested. If you tick the 'No' box move on to Q13 below.

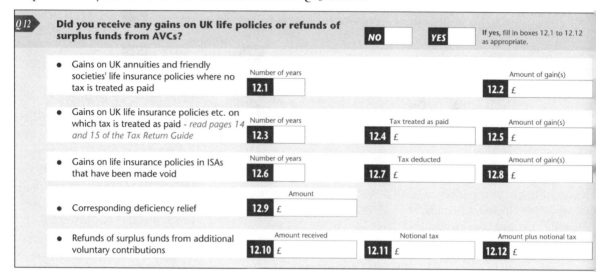

FILL THIS IN IF:

You made gains on UK annuities, life insurance policies or those in ISAs that have been made void, or you received a repayment from a FSAVC pension scheme.

WHERE TO FIND THE INFORMATION

The insurance company or scheme's trustees will have given you a statement containing the figures.

What to enter

In the case of life policies, the relevant number of years, notional tax and amounts received as shown on the insurance company's statement; for AVC refunds, the amounts received and notional tax figures.

Q13 Miscellaneous income

If you received any other income not covered in your tax return, then tick the 'Yes' box. Such income could include casual work, insurance or mail-order commission, royalties, accrued income charges, post-cessation receipts, etc. If you tick 'No' then move on to Q14.

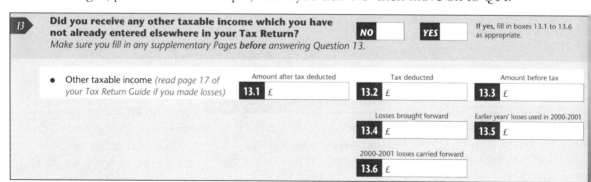

Read the information boxes on the next page to see what you need to include.

The following notes apply to Q13 of the tax return reproduced on the previous page.

FILL THIS IN IF:	**WHERE TO FIND THE INFORMATION**	**What to enter**

FILL THIS IN IF:

You received any miscellaneous income not declared anywhere else in your tax return or you have losses to be recorded.

WHERE TO FIND THE INFORMATION

Statements, receipts, invoices, contract notes, etc.

What to enter

The amount received in the year ended 5 April 2001 *after* claiming any allowable expenses (see page 34).

If tax has been deducted this must be shown. If you have losses brought forward, or you are creating a loss in this year, then these amounts must also be shown.

TAX TIP:

If you prefer, you can have post-cessation receipts taxed in the year in which the business ceased, in which case don't complete this section but tick box 23.5 (see page 26).

Having dealt with all forms of income, the tax return now offers you the opportunity to claim various reliefs, that is, amounts paid out which are allowable for tax and will reduce your tax bill.

Q14 Relief for pension contributions

If you are a member of your employer's pension scheme and no other scheme and all your contributions have been deducted at source, then tick the 'No' box and move to Q15. (You will get tax relief on these contributions deducted under PAYE.) Tick the 'Yes' box if you want to claim relief for other pension-scheme contributions.

RELIEFS *for the year ended 5 April 2001*

Q14 **Do you want to claim relief for pension contributions?**
Do not include contributions deducted from your pay by your employer to their pension scheme or associated AVC scheme, because tax relief is given automatically. But do include your contributions to personal pension schemes and Free-Standing AVC schemes.

NO ☐   **YES** ☐   If yes, fill in boxes 14.1 to 14.17 as appropriate.

■ *Retirement annuity contracts*

Qualifying payments made in 2000-2001	**14.1** £	2000-2001 payments used in an earlier year	**14.2** £	Relief claimed box 14.1 *minus* (boxes 14.2 and 14.3, but not 14.4)
2000-2001 payments now to be carried back	**14.3** £	Payments brought back from 2001-2002	**14.4** £	**14.5** £

■ *Self-employed contributions to personal pension plans*

Qualifying payments made in 2000-2001	**14.6** £	2000-2001 payments used in an earlier year	**14.7** £	Relief claimed box 14.6 *minus* (boxes 14.7 and 14.8, but not 14.9)
2000-2001 payments now to be carried back	**14.8** £	Payments brought back from 2001-2002	**14.9** £	**14.10** £

■ *Employee contributions to personal pension plans* (*include your gross contribution* - *see the note on box 14.11 in your Tax Return Guide*)

Qualifying payments made in 2000-2001 **14.11** £	2000-2001 payments used in an earlier year **14.12** £	Relief claimed
2000-2001 payments now to be carried back **14.13** £	Payments brought back from 2001-2002 **14.14** £	box 14.11 *minus* (boxes 14.12 and 14.13, but not 14.14) **14.15** £

■ *Contributions to other pension schemes and Free-Standing AVC schemes*

● Amount of contributions to employer's schemes **not deducted** at source from pay   **14.16** £

● Gross amount of Free-Standing Additional Voluntary Contributions paid in 2000-2001   **14.17** £

See also boxes 14.1 to 14.10 on the previous page.

WHERE TO FIND THE INFORMATION

The insurance company will provide a certificate of payments at the end of each tax year.

FILL THIS IN IF:

You have a retirement annuity policy or personal pension plan.

What to enter

The amounts paid in the year ended 5 April 2001.

There are boxes to complete if you wish the pension contributions to be carried back to the 1999–2000 tax year, or if you have already made a separate claim to carry back contributions.

You can carry back to 2000–2001 any payments made in the year ended 5 April 2002 if you paid prior to your tax return being submited, otherwise you will have to write to your tax office to advise them. Only fill in the box for qualifying payments if you are claiming higher-rate tax relief.

Only enter contributions in box 14.16 in the exceptional case of your employer not having deducted them from your salary before calculating PAYE.

REMEMBER:

As from April 2001, if you have paid contributions in excess of the maximum allowance for the year to 5 April 2001, you cannot carry forward unused reliefs if you have paid less than maximum contributions in the previous six years. The table below shows the maximum contributions allowable for tax as a percentage of your earnings.

Maximum contributions allowable for tax as a percentage of your earnings

Age at beginning of tax year	Retirement annuity premium %	Personal pension plan %
up to 35	17.5	17.5
36 to 45	17.5	20.0
46 to 50	17.5	25.0
51 to 55	20.0	30.0
56 to 60	22.5	35.0
61 to 74	27.5	40.0

For pension scheme plans taken out after 14 March 1989 the maximum net relevant earnings figures on which relief is available are as follows:

From 6 April:

1993	£75,000	1997	£84,000
1994	£76,800	1998	£87,600
1995	£78,600	1999	£90,600
1996	£82,200	2000	£91,800

The figure from 6 April 2001 will be £95,400.

Q15 Other reliefs you can claim

Tick the 'Yes' box if you want to claim for vocational training undertaken outside the UK, interest paid on qualifying loans, Venture Capital Trust and Enterprise Investment Scheme subscriptions, gifts of money or investments made to charities, post-cessation expenses, annuities or payments to a trade union or friendly society for death benefits.

  If you do not wish to claim any of these, tick the 'No' box and move to Q16.

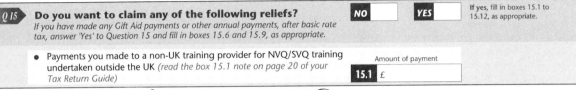

Q15 ▸ **Do you want to claim any of the following reliefs?** **NO** [ ] **YES** [ ] If yes, fill in boxes 15.1 to 15.12, as appropriate.

If you have made any Gift Aid payments or other annual payments, after basic rate tax, answer 'Yes' to Question 15 and fill in boxes 15.6 and 15.9, as appropriate.

- Payments you made to a non-UK training provider for NVQ/SVQ training undertaken outside the UK *(read the box 15.1 note on page 20 of your Tax Return Guide)*   Amount of payment **15.1** £

FILL THIS IN IF:

You have paid for a vocational training course leading to a NVQ or SVQ qualification provided by a non-UK training provider undertaken outside the UK. Telephone 0151 472 6022 for help with any queries.

WHERE TO FIND THE INFORMATION

The training organisation will have given you a certificate confirming the payment made.

What to enter

Normally you will have paid your training provider after deducting tax at basic rate, in which case leave 15.1 blank.

  If tax has not been deducted, contact your provider for a retrospective reimbursement.

  You should not complete this section if the course was undertaken primarily as a leisure activity.

- Interest eligible for relief on qualifying loans   Amount of payment **15.2** £

FILL THIS IN IF:

You pay interest on a loan which was used to buy shares in, or lend to:

  a closely controlled trading company where you own more than 5 per cent of the company's shares, or, if less, have worked for the greater part of your time in the management of the company – such interest is not allowed for tax if a claim for relief has been made under the Enterprise Investment Scheme;

  a partnership or employee-controlled company;

  a co-operative, provided that you work in it full time.

Or you pay interest on a loan to pay inheritance tax or buy plant or machinery for business use.

Or you pay interest on a loan to buy an annuity if the person buying the annuity is aged 65 or over when the loan is secured on the individual's main residence in the UK or Republic of Ireland and the loan was taken out before 9 March 1999 (or other loans have replaced the original loan). Relief for these loans is restricted to 22 per cent. You can request help sheet IR340 for more information about what you can claim. There is also an Inland Revenue helpline – 0151 472 6155.

WHERE TO FIND THE INFORMATION

Ask the lender for a certificate of interest from which you can obtain the figures to go in your return.

What to enter

The gross amount actually paid, but there is no need to enter a figure in respect of loan interest to buy an annuity if relief has been given under MIRAS.

Do not include any interest in box 15.2 on a loan to purchase let property; this should be entered in box 5.26 in the Land and Property return (see page 45).

Interest on loans to buy your main home is no longer allowed as a tax deduction.

	Amount claimed up to £2,000	
• Maintenance or alimony payments you have made under a court order, Child Support Agency assessment or legally binding order or agreement *(see page 21 of your Tax Return Guide)*	**15.3** £	

FILL THIS IN IF:

You, or your former husband or wife, was born before 6 April 1935 and you make legally enforceable maintenance or alimony payments. Do not include voluntary payments for there is no tax relief for these.

WHERE TO FIND THE INFORMATION

You will know from your own records or from a court, DSS or Child Support Agency statement the payments made.

What to enter

In box 15.3 state the amount you paid in the year ended 5 April 2001. The maximum figure for tax relief is £2,000 so you can only claim £2,000 or the amount you actually paid, whichever is the lower.

If your former husband or wife has remarried in 2000–2001 the relief ceases from the date of the marriage.

	Amount on which relief is claimed
• Subscriptions for Venture Capital Trust shares (up to £100,000)	**15.4** £
• Subscriptions under the Enterprise Investment Scheme (up to £150,000)	**15.5** £

FILL THIS IN IF:

You have subscribed for shares in a Venture Capital Trust or an EIS.

WHERE TO FIND THE INFORMATION

The trust or scheme will have given you a share certificate and a memorandum of the trust's status, etc. and a receipt for the amount paid.

In the case of the EIS you will receive a form EIS 3 or EIS 5, which the tax office may wish to see to support your claim.

What to enter

The amount you subscribed up to the maximum.

	Amount on which relief is claimed
● Gift Aid and payments under charitable covenants	**15.6** £

FILL THIS IN IF:

You have signed a covenant prior to 6 April 2000 to pay money to a charity for a period of at least four years
OR
You have donated money to a charity and signed a Gift Aid certificate R190(SD)
OR
You have donated £100 or more, including gifts made by instalments once they reach £100, to the Millennium Gift Aid between April 2000 and 31 December 2000.

WHERE TO FIND THE INFORMATION

You should have a copy of the covenant form you signed, or a note of the payments made, or a Gift Aid declaration form from the charity confirming the amount paid.

What to enter

The net amount of the actual payments made. You will be regarded as having deducted tax at basic rate before making the payments, so further tax relief is only available if you are a higher-rate taxpayer.

	Amount of relief claimed
● Gifts of qualifying investments to charities	**15.7** £

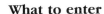

FILL THIS IN IF:

You have have gifted qualifying investments to a UK charity or you have sold such investments to a charity for less than their market value.

WHERE TO FIND THE INFORMATION

Contract notes transferring the investments.

What to enter

The total value, at the time of transfer, of all the investments given or sold to charities in the year ended 5 April 2001. You must deduct any consideration or value actually received by you (if any) and also deduct any costs involved (brokers' fees, stamp duty, etc.).

- Post-cessation expenses, pre-incorporation losses brought forward and losses on relevant discounted securities, etc. *(see page 22 of your Tax Return Guide)*

Amount of payment

15.8 £

What to enter
The amount of the relevant expenditure.

FILL THIS IN IF:

You ceased trading within the last seven years but have still incurred expenditure closely related to that business, or you have losses carried forward from self-employment and you transfer your business to a company. Losses on discounted securities are also entered here and any pre-incorporation losses.

WHERE TO FIND THE INFORMATION

From invoices, receipts, correspondence, etc.

REMEMBER:

If your income in the year of payment of post-cessation expenses is not sufficient to utilise the relief fully, then a claim may be made for the excess to be treated as an allowable loss for capital gains tax purposes (see page 49).

- Annuities

Amount on which relief is claimed

15.9 £

FILL THIS IN IF:

You have paid annuities or covenants for genuine commercial reasons in connection with your trade or profession.

WHERE TO FIND THE INFORMATION

Annuity statements or copies of the covenant form.

What to enter
The amount actually paid in the year ended 5 April 2001. These payments are treated as having been made after basic rate tax has been deducted – further relief will only be due if you are a higher-rate taxpayer.

REMINDER:

With self assessment tax legislation, the law requires you to keep all records of earnings, income, benefits, profits, expenses, etc. and all other relevant information for 22 months from the end of the tax year if you are employed, and for 5 years and 10 months if you are self-employed.

	Half amount of payment
• Payments to a trade union or friendly society for death benefits	**15.10** £

FILL THIS IN IF:	WHERE TO FIND THE INFORMATION
You make compulsory payments to provide annuities for widows and orphans where relief is not given by your employer, or if part of your trade union subscription relates to a pension, insurance or funeral benefit, or you have a friendly society policy providing sickness and death benefits (the part relating to death benefit may qualify for tax relief).	The company or trade union operating the policies will provide you each year with a statement that will give you the figures required.

What to enter

One half of the payment made relating to superannuation, life assurance, funeral or death benefit.

	Relief claimed
• Payment to your employer's compulsory widow's, widower's or orphan's benefit scheme *(available in some circumstances – **first** read the notes on page 23 of your Tax Return Guide)*	**15.11** £

FILL THIS IN IF:	WHERE TO FIND THE INFORMATION
These payments are compulsory and relief was not totally given under PAYE.	The statement from your employer or the scheme's trustees.

What to enter
The lower of £100 or 22 per cent of the amount not relieved under PAYE.

	Relief claimed
• Relief claimed on a qualifying distribution on the **redemption** of bonus shares or securities.	**15.12** £

FILL THIS IN IF:	WHERE TO FIND THE INFORMATION
You receive bonus securities or shares.	The contract notes or offer document.

What to enter
This is a very complicated calculation. Refer to the tax return guide page 23. Ring orderline 0845 9000 404 if you do not have a copy.

Q16 Your tax allowances for the year ending 5 April 2001

You automatically get the personal allowance each year if you are resident in the UK but all other allowances have to be claimed.

If you want to claim blind person's allowance, married couple's allowance, widow's bereavement allowance or you wish to transfer surplus allowances between husband and wife, then tick the 'Yes' box. Otherwise tick the 'No' box and proceed to Q17.

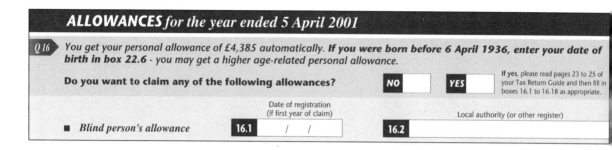

ALLOWANCES *for the year ended 5 April 2001*

Q 16 *You get your personal allowance of £4,385 automatically.* **If you were born before 6 April 1936, enter your date of birth in box 22.6** *- you may get a higher age-related personal allowance.*

Do you want to claim any of the following allowances?   NO   YES   If yes, please read pages 23 to 25 of your Tax Return Guide and then fill in boxes 16.1 to 16.18 as appropriate.

Date of registration (if first year of claim)   Local authority (or other register)

■ *Blind person's allowance*   **16.1** / /   **16.2**

FILL THIS IN IF:

You are a registered blind person.

What to enter

The date you were registered blind if it is the first time you have claimed, and also the name of your local authority.

TAX TIP:

This allowance is also claimable by blind persons in the year *preceding* the year in which they were officially registered as blind if, at the end of the previous year, evidence was *then* available to support the eventual registration application.

■ *Married couple's allowance* - *In 2000-2001 married couple's allowance can only be claimed if either you, or your husband or wife, were born* **before 6 April 1935.** *So you can only claim the allowance in 2000-2001 if either of you had reached* **65 years of age before 6 April 2000.** *Further guidance is given beginning on page 23 of your Tax Return Guide.*

If **both** you and your husband or wife were born after 5 April 1935 you cannot claim; **do not** complete boxes 16.3 to 16.13.

If you can claim fill in boxes 16.3 and 16.4 if you are a married man or if you are a married woman and you are claiming half or all of the married couple's allowance.

● Enter your date of birth (if born before 6 April 1935)   **16.3** / /

● Enter your spouse's date of birth (**if born before 6 April 1935 and** if older than you)   **16.4** / /

Then, if you are a married man fill in boxes 16.5 to 16.9. If you are a married woman fill in boxes 16.10 to 16.13.

• Wife's full name	**16.5**		• Date of marriage (if after 5 April 2000)	**16.6** / /
• Tick box 16.7 if you or your wife have allocated half the allowance to her				**16.7**
• Tick box 16.8 if you and your wife have allocated all the allowance to her				**16.8**
• Enter in box 16.9 the date of birth of any previous wife with whom you lived at any time during 2000-2001. *Read 'Special rules if you are a man who married in the year ended 5 April 2001' on page 25 before completing box 16.9.*				**16.9** / /
• Tick box 16.10 if you or your husband have allocated half the allowance to you				**16.10**
• Tick box 16.11 if you and your husband have allocated all the allowance to you				**16.11**
• Husband's full name	**16.12**		• Date of marriage (if after 5 April 2000)	**16.13** / /

FILL THIS IN IF:

Either you, or your husband or wife, were born before 6 April 1935. (If both of you were born after this date, you cannot claim the married couple's allowance.)

What to enter

Your date of birth in 16.3 and your wife or husband's date of birth, if older than you, in 16.4.

If you are a married man fill in boxes 16.5 to 16.9 with ticks or date of birth – married women should similarly fill in boxes 16.10 to 16.13.

TAX TIP:

Who gets the married couple's allowance?

The allowance automatically goes to the husband unless either the husband or the wife has asked for one half to be given to each other (boxes 16.8 and 16.10) or both husband and wife have asked for the whole allowance to be given to the wife (boxes 16.8 and 16.11).

With the abolition of the married couple's allowance from 6 April 2000 for younger couples, this allowance will only apply in future to those couples where either the husband or wife was aged 65 or over on or before 5 April 2000.

It is beneficial to transfer this allowance if it cannot be used fully by a husband. Ask your tax office for Form 18 if you wish to transfer half, or all, of the married couple's allowance, but this has to be submitted before the tax year to which it relates so it is already too late for it to apply to the 2001–2002 tax year but see page 24 regarding surplus allowances.

ANOTHER TAX TIP:

The age-allowance trap

If you are married, over 65 and claiming age allowance, estimate your total income for the next tax year to see that no personal allowance will remain unused; it may be beneficial to transfer savings, etc. into joint names.

■ *Widow's bereavement allowance* - *see page 25 of your Tax Return Guide before completing box 16.14.*

● Date of your husband's death | 16.14 | / | / |

FILL THIS IN IF:

If you are a widow and your husband died in the twelve months ended 6 April 2000 and you have not remarried in that year.

What to enter
The date of your husband's death.

■ *Transfer of surplus allowances* - *see page 25 of your Tax Return Guide before you fill in boxes 16.15 to 16.18.*

● Tick box 16.15 if you want your spouse to have your unused allowances | 16.15 |

● Tick box 16.16 if you want to have your spouse's unused allowances | 16.16 |

Please give details in the 'Additional information' box, box 23.6, on page 8 - *see page 25 of your Tax Return Guide for what is needed.*

If you want to calculate your tax, enter the amount of the surplus allowance you can have.

● Blind person's **surplus** allowance | 16.17 | £ |

● Married couple's **surplus** allowance | 16.18 | £ |

FILL THIS IN IF:

You are unable to use all your married couple's allowance or blind person's allowance and wish to transfer the surplus to your husband or wife.

What to enter
If you have surplus allowances to transfer, tick box 16.15, and if you are claiming surplus allowances, tick box 16.16. You may also add your calculation of the surplus allowances available in boxes 16.17 and 16.18 if you wish.

Q17 Student loan repayments

Repayment of student loans made to a new borrower from August 1998 is now collected via the tax system. These loans are called 'Income Contingent'. Tick the 'Yes' box if the student loan company told you repayment commenced in the year ended 5 April 2001. Otherwise, tick the 'No' box and move on to Q18.

 Are you liable to make Student Loan Repayments for 2000-2001 on an Income Contingent Student Loan?
Read the note on page 25 of your Tax Return Guide.

| NO | | YES | |

If yes, and you are calculating your tax enter in box 18.2A the amount you work out is repayable in 2000-2001.

Q18 Do you want to calculate your tax and any student loan repayment?

If you do **not** want to calculate your own tax liability or tax refund and you would prefer the tax office to do it for you, just tick 'No' and go on to Q19.

If you **do** want to do it yourself, then tick 'Yes' and complete the boxes as shown.

OTHER INFORMATION *for the year ended 5 April 2001*

18	Do you want to calculate your tax and any Student Loan Repayment?	NO	YES	If yes, do it now and then fill in boxes 18.1 to 18.8. Your Tax Calculation Guide will help.

- Unpaid tax for earlier years **included in your tax code for 2000-2001** — 18.1 £
- Tax due for 2000-2001 included in your tax code for a later year — 18.2 £
- Student Loan Repayment due — 18.2A £
- Total tax, Class 4 NIC and Student Loan Repayment due for 2000-2001 **before** you made any payments on account *(put the amount in brackets if an overpayment)* — 18.3 £
- Tax due for earlier years — 18.4 £
- Tick box 18.5 if you have calculated tax overpaid for earlier years and enter the amount in the 'Additional information' box, box 23.6 on page 8. — 18.5
- Your first payment on account for 2001-2002 *(include the pence)* — 18.6 £
  Tick box 18.7 if you are making a claim to reduce your 2001-2002 payments on account and say why in the 'Additional information' box, box 23.6, on page 8 — 18.7
- Tick box 18.8 if you are reclaiming any 2001-2002 tax now and enter the amount in the 'Additional information' box, box 23.6 on page 8. — 18.8

FILL THIS IN IF:
You want to calculate your own tax.

What to enter
You need to turn to page 62 of this book for a tax calculation summary, then you can complete boxes 18.1 to 18.8.

Q19 Do you want to claim a tax repayment?

If you are due a tax repayment of more than £10 and you **don't** want it offset against your next tax bill, or through your PAYE code number, then tick 'Yes' and fill in the information requested - otherwise tick 'No'. If you do not claim a repayment but one is due to you, then the tax office will set any amount to be refunded against your next tax bill. Now proceed to Q20 and Q21.

19	Do you want to claim a repayment if you have paid too **much tax?** *(If you tick 'No' or the tax you have overpaid is below £10, I will use the amount you are owed to reduce your next tax bill.)*	NO	YES	If yes, fill in boxes 19.1A to 19.12 as appropriate.

Should the repayment be sent:
- direct to your bank or building society account? *Tick box 19.1A and fill in boxes 19.3 to 19.7* **19.1A**
- by cheque to you at your home address? *Tick box 19.1B* **19.1B**

or
- to a nominee? *Tick box 19.2, fill in boxes 19.3 to 19.11, as appropriate, and box 19.12* **19.2**

Fill in boxes 19.3 to 19.7 if the repayment is to be sent to your own, or your nominees' bank or building society account

Name of bank or building society	**19.3**	
Branch sort code	**19.4**	— —
Account number	**19.5**	
Name of account holder	**19.6**	
Building society ref.	**19.7**	

- If your nominee is your agent, *tick box 19.8* **19.8**

Agent's reference for you (if your nominee is your agent) **19.9**

Name of your nominee/agent

I authorise **19.10**

Nominee/agent address **19.11**

Postcode

to receive on my behalf the amount due

This authority must be signed by you. A photocopy of your signature will not do. **19.12** Signature

Q20 Tax refunds, etc.

Tick the 'Yes' box if you have received a tax refund from the tax office or Benefits Agency in the year ended 5 April 2001, or notification of any refund reallocated to other tax liabilities and state the amount. If 'No', proceed to Q21.

Q 20	Have you already had any 2000-2001 tax refunded or set off by your Inland Revenue office or the Benefits Agency (in Northern Ireland, the Social Security Agency)? *Read the notes on page 26 of your Tax Return Guide*	NO	YES	If yes, enter the amount of the refund in box 20.1.
				20.1 £

Q21 and Q22 Check your personal details

Check that your name, address and reference number on the front page of your tax form are correct and tick Q21, then proceed to Q22. You do not **have** to state a telephone number but it could save the tax office and you having to write letters to sort out a minor problem or misunderstanding.

Q 21	Are your name or address on the front of the Tax Return wrong?	NO	YES	If yes, please make any corrections on the front of the form.

Q 22 **Please give other personal details in boxes 22.1 to 22.7.** *This information helps us to be more efficient and effective and may support claims you have made elsewhere in your Tax Return*

Please give a daytime telephone number if convenient. It is often simpler to phone if we need to ask you about your Tax Return.

Your telephone number
22.1

or, if you prefer, your agent's telephone number
22.2

and their name and address
22.3

Postcode

Enter your first two forenames
22.4

Say if you are single, married, widowed, divorced or separated
22.5

Enter your date of birth
22.6 / /

Enter your National Insurance number (if known)
22.7

Q23 and Q24 Additional information and declaration

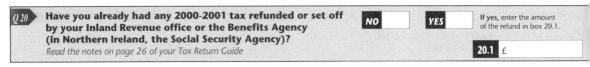

OTHER INFORMATION *for the year ended 5 April 2001, continued*

Q 23 **Please tick boxes 23.1 to 23.5 if they apply. Provide any additional information in box 23.6 below.**

Tick box 23.1 if you expect to receive a new pension or new Social Security benefit in 2001-2002.	**23.1**
Tick box 23.2 if you do **not** want any tax you owe for 2000-2001 collected through your tax code.	**23.2**
Tick box 23.3 if this Tax Return contains figures that are provisional because you do not yet have final figures. Page 26 of your Tax Return Guide explains the circumstances in which Tax Returns containing provisional figures may be accepted and tells you what you must enter in box 23.6 below.	**23.3**
Tick box 23.4 if you are claiming relief now for 2001-2002 trading, or certain capital, losses. Enter in box 23.6 the amount and year.	**23.4**
Tick box 23.5 if you are claiming: • to have post-cessation or other business receipts taxed as income of an earlier year. Enter in box 23.6 the amount and year • backwards or forwards spreading of literary or artistic income. Enter in box 23.6 details of any amounts spread back to last year and, if appropriate, the year before.	**23.5**

23.6 *Additional information*

Your tax office needs all the information in order to ensure that your tax affairs are dealt with efficiently; if there is insufficient room, use the additional information box on page 8 of the form.

You must then sign and date the Declaration Q24 ensuring that you have ticked the boxes to indicate which sections of the tax return you have completed and are returning.

REMINDER:

With self assessment tax legislation, the law requires you to keep all records of earnings, income, benefits, profits, expenses, etc. and all other relevant information for 22 months from the end of the tax year if you are employed, and for 5 years and 10 months if you are self-employed.

Q 24 | **Declaration**

I have filled in and am sending back to you the following pages:

	Tick			Tick			Tick
1 TO 8 OF THIS FORM							
EMPLOYMENT			PARTNERSHIP			TRUSTS, ETC	
SHARE SCHEMES			LAND & PROPERTY			CAPITAL GAINS	
SELF-EMPLOYMENT			FOREIGN			NON-RESIDENCE, ETC	

Before you send your completed Tax Return back to your Inland Revenue office, you must sign the statement below. If you give false information or conceal any part of your income or chargeable gains, you may be liable to financial penalties and/or you may be prosecuted.

24.1 The information I have given in this Tax Return is correct and complete to the best of my knowledge and belief.

Signature   Date

If you are signing for someone else please read the notes on page 27 of the Tax Return Guide, and:

• state the capacity in which you are signing (for example, as executor or receiver)

24.2

• give the name of the person you are signing for and **your** name and address in box 23.6 above.

TAX TIP:

Many tax returns, particularly those being sent in after 30 September last year, were unsigned and this means that the return is wrongly submitted and not complete. This could waste time and cost you interest and penalties. Make sure you sign it!

What to do when you have completed your tax return

Sign the return and keep a copy

When you sign your tax return you are declaring that to the best of your knowledge and belief the return is complete, true and accurate.

It is often thought that if you keep quiet about some of your income, then the tax inspector will not find out about it. This is not the case. The tax authorities have many sources of information, the most common being your employer, banks, building societies and other businesses, all of whom may be required to make a return of payments made to individuals and businesses. If you forget to include some of your income on the form you should immediately notify your tax office explaining your error.

REMEMBER:

You will only have entered **total** figures in the boxes on your tax return, so ensure that you keep a note of how you arrived at the figures – the tax office may ask for them. Use the tax organiser at the end of this book.

TAX TIP:

Do not worry if you have forgotten to claim an allowance due to you, for you have a time limit of six years in which to tell your tax office of your mistake. Therefore you can go back to 6 April 1993 to check your tax and possibly get a rebate – and interest too.

You should keep a copy of your completed tax return form so that, at a later date, you can check your PAYE code or the amount of tax you have paid. If you fill in the tax forms reproduced in this book you will have a permanent record.

When to send in your tax return

If you don't want to calculate your own tax:

You need to send in your tax return by 30 September 2001 – the tax office should then send you a statement by 31 January 2002. This form, SA302 'Self assessment – Tax Calculation for 2000–2001' will either agree your figures or identify corrections that the tax office have made. If you disagree with the tax office's comments write to them; otherwise pay the amount demanded.

If you do want to calculate your own tax:

If you wish to use the tax calculator and calculate your own tax liability (see page 62) then you have until 31 January 2002 to send in your return, in which case you should also pay the tax that you think is due.

If you miss the date?

If you send in your return after 30 September 2001 (and *you* don't want to calculate your own tax) the tax office will not guarantee to calculate it for you before 31 January; they will still send you, however, a demand for a payment on account on 31 January, so *you* need to know approximately what your tax liability is in total.

Payments on account

f you have enough untaxed income, or are self-employed, you will have to make two payments on account for each tax year, e.g. for the year ended 5 April 2001 the first payment or 50 per cent of your expected tax bill on 31 January 2001 and the second 50 per cent on 1 July 2001; any balance due once your tax liability is agreed is payable on 31 January 2002. f there is a tax refund due, your tax office will deal with it fairly quickly. (Self-employed payments will also include Class 4 National Insurance liability.) It is up to you to work out how nuch you need to pay on account, although your tax office will normally send you an 'on ccount' statement once your pattern of income is established.

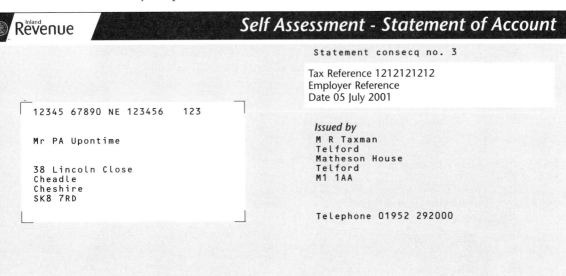

Inland Revenue

Self Assessment - Statement of Account

Statement consecq no. 3

Tax Reference 1212121212
Employer Reference
Date 05 July 2001

12345 67890 NE 123456   123

Mr PA Upontime

38 Lincoln Close
Cheadle
Cheshire
SK8 7RD

Issued by
M R Taxman
Telford
Matheson House
Telford
M1 1AA

Telephone 01952 292000

This statement shows the position of your account

Date	Transaction	Amount	Balance
	Balance of account at 05 JUL 01		0.00
Becoming due 31 JUL 01	2nd Payment on account due for year 00-01	2000.00	2000.00

This statement reminds you that an amount becomes due shortly.
Please make sure that payment reaches us by the date it is due.
You will be charged interest if you pay late.

SA300

What to do with this form

Form SA300 above is an example of a demand for payment of tax – either on account or for a specific tax liability. If you agree with the figure, you should pay the amount by the date shown otherwise you could incur interest payments (see page 5). If it is wrong, ask for form SA303 (see page 30).

Inland Revenue | **Self Assessment** | **Claim to reduce payments on account**

If this reference box is blank please give your Tax reference, Employer reference or National Insurance number. You will find this information, together with the name and address of your Tax Office, in the top right hand corner of your Statement of Account.	Tax reference Employer reference National Insurance number

Tax Office name and address

Please read the notes overleaf before completing this form

Name of taxpayer

Tax year to which this claim relates [—]   *Example, enter the tax year ending 5 April 1999 as* | 1998 — 99 |

I believe that

√ ☐ the total Income Tax and Class 4 NIC payable for the tax year of claim (less any tax deducted at source and tax credits on dividends) will be less than the total of the payments on account based on the liability for the previous tax year

or

√ ☐ there will be no liability to any Income Tax or Class 4 NIC for the tax year of claim

My reason(s)
√

☐ the taxable business profits for the tax year of claim are less than in the previous tax year

☐ the tax allowances and reliefs for the tax year of claim are more than in the previous tax year

☐ the tax deducted at source for the tax year of claim is more than in the previous tax year

☐ the taxable income (after allowances) for the tax year of claim is less than in the previous tax year

☐ other reason *please specify*

I wish to reduce each of the payments on account for the tax year of claim to £ [   ]

*Each reduced payment on account should be **half** of the net Income Tax and Class 4 NIC you expect to have to pay for the tax year.*

I understand that

• **if the payments on account finally due are greater than the amounts paid, interest will be payable on the difference**

• **any incorrect statement made fraudulently or negligently in connection with this claim could incur a penalty.**

Date [   ]

Signed [   ]

Agent's Name *if signed by agent* [   ]

Agent's Reference [   ]

When you have completed and signed this form send it to your Tax Office.

FILL THIS IN IF:

You wish to reduce the amount of tax and national insurance being demanded on account. You must fill in the appropriate boxes on this form so that the tax office understand why you are claiming a reduction. Send the completed form to your tax office, together with a cheque for the revised payment on account.

Your tax return – supplementary pages

EMPLOYMENT

You need to fill in this part of the tax return if you were employed. It will cover your income and benefits from employment and your claim for expenses for the year ended 5 April 2001. You must use a separate form for each employment. (Ministers of Religion and Members of Parliament have different versions of this form.)

Income for the year ended 5 April 2001

Inland Revenue

EMPLOYMENT

Details of employer

Employer's PAYE reference - may be shown under 'Tax Office number and reference' on your P60 or 'PAYE reference' on your P45

1.1

Employer's name

1.2

Date employment started
(only if between 6 April 2000 and 5 April 2001)

1.3 / /

Employer's address

1.5

Date finished (only if between 6 April 2000 and 5 April 2001)

1.4 / /

Tick box 1.6 if you were a director of the company

1.6

and, if so, tick box 1.7 if it was a close company

1.7

Postcode

Income from employment

■ *Money* - *see Notes, page EN3*

Before tax

● Payments from P60 (or P45)

1.8 £

● Payments not on P60 etc. - tips

1.9 £

- other payments (excluding expenses entered below and lump sums and compensation payments or benefits entered overleaf)

1.10 £

Tax deducted

● UK tax deducted from payments in boxes 1.8 to 1.10

1.11 £

WHERE TO FIND THE INFORMATION

By law, your employer has to give you a P60 form (certificate of pay, income tax and national insurance) by 31 May 2001 (see page 56). This will show the earnings figures to go in your tax return, and the tax deducted. Alternatively, you may need to refer to a P45 form or your pay slips.

FILL THIS IN IF:

You are an employee or a director, and receive a salary, wages, fees or benefits.

What to enter

Fill in boxes 1.1 to 1.7 with the information requested. In box 1.8 show the amount you have received *before* any deductions for income tax or National Insurance.

You *are* allowed to subtract any deduction made by your employer for contributions to an approved pension scheme or payroll giving donations.

Enter in box 1.9 any tips or gratuities you have received if they are *not* included in the figure in box 1.8.

Box 1.10 is for any other payments, although most of them will be specifically referred to later in this form.

Enter any tax deducted in box 1.11.

■ **Benefits and expenses** - *see Notes, pages EN3 to EN6. If any benefits connected with termination of employment were received, or enjoyed, after that termination and were from a **former** employer you need to complete Help Sheet IR204, available from the Orderline. Do not enter such benefits here.*

● Assets transferred/ payments made for you | Amount **1.12** £

● Vans | Amount **1.18** £

● Vouchers, credit cards and tokens | Amount **1.13** £

● Interest-free and low-interest loans | Amount **1.19** £

● Living accommodation | Amount **1.14** £

box 1.20 is not used

● Mileage allowance | Amount **1.15** £

● Private medical or dental insurance | Amount **1.21** £

● Company cars | Amount **1.16** £

● Other benefits | Amount **1.22** £

● Fuel for company cars | Amount **1.17** £

● Expenses payments received and balancing charges | Amount **1.23** £

WHERE TO FIND THE INFORMATION

Most of the information will be found on the P11D form, a copy of which your employer must give you by 6 July 2001. For an explanation of how car and fuel benefits are calculated, see page 59.

FILL THIS IN IF:

You have received any 'benefits' from your employer. Typically those might include private health cover or a low-interest loan.

or

Your employer has provided you, or your family, with a car available for your private use.

or

Your employer has either paid directly or reimbursed any expenses relating to your employment, not covered by a 'dispensation'.

To find out if your benefit is taxable, refer to page 61 of this book.

Is the benefit taxable?

All directors and those employees whose earnings, including expenses and benefits in kind, are at a rate of £8,500 or more a year are liable to pay tax on benefits and expenses received.

Certain benefits are taxable on all employees.

The car benefit tax applies to all company cars, including those that are leased.

See page 34 for tax relief you can claim in respect of genuine business expenditure.

What to enter

The amount paid to you as a benefit or expense or the taxable value.

If your employer has agreed with the tax office that certain expenses need not be shown as you would be entitled to tax relief for the full amount (e.g. representatives' overnight stays; mileage allowances for your own car used on business), then your employer should give you details of the expenses covered by the arrangement.

Income from employment continued

■ *Lump sums and compensation payments or benefits including such payments and benefits from a former employer*
Note that 'lump sums' here includes any contributions which your employer made to an unapproved retirement benefits scheme

You must read page EN6 of the Notes **before** filling in boxes 1.24 to 1.30

Reliefs

- £30,000 exemption **1.24** £
- Foreign service and disability **1.25** £
- Retirement and death lump sums **1.26** £

Taxable lump sums

- From box B of *Help Sheet IR204* **1.27** £
- From box K of *Help Sheet IR204* **1.28** £
- From box L of *Help Sheet IR204* **1.29** £

Tax deducted
- Tax deducted from payments in boxes 1.27 to 1.29 **1.30** £

FILL THIS IN IF:

You have been made redundant or dismissed with compensation.

WHERE TO FIND THE INFORMATION

You will find the information in a letter or statement from your employer.

What to enter

As this is a complicated subject you may need Inland Revenue help sheet IR204 to assist you in filling in these boxes. If it has not been sent, then telephone 0845 9000 404 for a copy.

DO NOT FILL THIS IN IF:

The amount you received has had tax deducted from it and it is included in the figures on your P60 form included in box 1.8 on page 31.

WARNING

If your contract of employment gives you a right to compensation on ceasing to be employed, then any lump sum you receive will be taxable, regardless of the amount.

Is it taxable?

The first £30,000 of compensation is tax free but any amount in excess of that figure is taxable at your highest individual rate of tax – but note the warning opposite.

■ *Foreign earnings not taxable in the UK in the year ended 5 April 2001* - see Notes, page EN6 **1.31** £

FILL THIS IN IF:

You are non-resident (see page 51) or have reason to believe such income is not liable to UK tax.

What to enter

That part of your income that you think is not taxable in the UK.

■ *Expenses you incurred in doing your job* - see Notes, pages EN6 to EN8

- Travel and subsistence costs — **1.32** £
- Fixed deductions for expenses — **1.33** £
- Professional fees and subscriptions — **1.34** £
- Other expenses and capital allowances — **1.35** £
- Tick box 1.36 if the figure in box 1.32 includes travel between your home and a permanent workplace — **1.36**

FILL THIS IN IF:

Your employer has reimbursed business expenses or you have paid an expense that has not been reimbursed by your employer without which you would have been unable to do your job properly (the tax law says the expense must be 'wholly, exclusively and necessary for your employment'). You may be able to get a letter from your employer confirming this fact.

TAX TIP:

Apart from those expenses referred to in the form, under 1.35 you could consider claiming for: Protective clothing and laundering costs, trade journals and technical books; The cost of business mileage travelled in your own car, bicycle or motorbike – see page 59; Use of a room at home set aside as an office based on a proportion of your costs if you *have* to do additional work at home.

What to enter

The amount of the expense in the appropriate box (see page 37 in respect of capital allowances). Travel between home and a permanent workplace is not allowed as a deduction.

■ *Foreign Earnings Deduction* (seafarers only) — **1.37** £

■ *Foreign tax for which tax credit relief not claimed* — **1.38** £

FILL THIS IN IF:

You are a seafarer.

WHERE TO FIND THE INFORMATION

The rules are very complicated so ask your tax office for help sheet IR2055 by ringing 0845 9000 444.

Student Loans

■ *Student Loans repaid by deduction by employer* - see Notes, page EN8 — **1.39** £

FILL THIS IN IF:

You had student loan repayments deducted by your employer.

WHERE TO FIND THE INFORMATION

Your P60 form and pay slips from a previous employer(s) if you had more than one job.

What to enter

The amount of loan repayment deducted from your earnings in the year.

SHARE SCHEMES

You need to fill in these pages if you received any share options or you were a member of an all-employee share ownership plan or you were granted Enterprise Management Incentive options.

Share options

Read the Notes, pages SN1 to SN8 **before** filling in the boxes

■ Approved savings-related share options

		Name of company and share scheme	Tick if shares unlisted	Taxable amount
● Exercise	2.1		2.2	2.3 £
● Cancellation or release	2.4		2.5	2.6 £

■ Approved discretionary share options

		Name of company and share scheme		
● Exercise	2.7		2.8	2.9 £
● Cancellation or release	2.10		2.11	2.12 £

■ Enterprise Management Incentive options

		Name of company and unique option reference		
● Exercise	2.13		2.14	2.15 £
● Cancellation or release	2.16		2.17	2.18 £

■ Unapproved share options

		Name of company and share scheme		
● Grant	2.19		2.20	2.21 £
● Exercise	2.22		2.23	2.24 £
● Cancellation or release	2.25		2.26	2.27 £

Approved all-employee share ownership plans

Read the Notes, page SN2, **before** filling in the boxes

		Name of company and share plan		
● Shares ceasing to be subject to the plan	2.28		2.29	2.30 £

TAX TIP:

The tax legislation governing share schemes generally has grown out of all proportion with each succeeding budget and this section now runs to four pages. Because of their complexity only the first section is shown above.

Schemes can vary considerably from employer to employer, and before filling in this part of the tax return you should ask for Inland Revenue help sheet IR 218 – telephone 0845 9000 404 if you require a copy – and also seek guidance from the trustees of your share scheme or your employer.

If you have made any capital gains or losses, do not enter them in this section – ask the tax office for Capital Gains supplementary pages by telephoning order line 0845 9000 404.

SELF-EMPLOYMENT

You need to fill in this part of the tax return if you were self-employed but not in a partnership. (If you were in a partnership, then you need the Partnership supplementary pages – see page 42).

Telephone the Inland Revenue order line on 0845 9000 404 if you need either of the forms – you need to fill in a separate set of pages for each business.

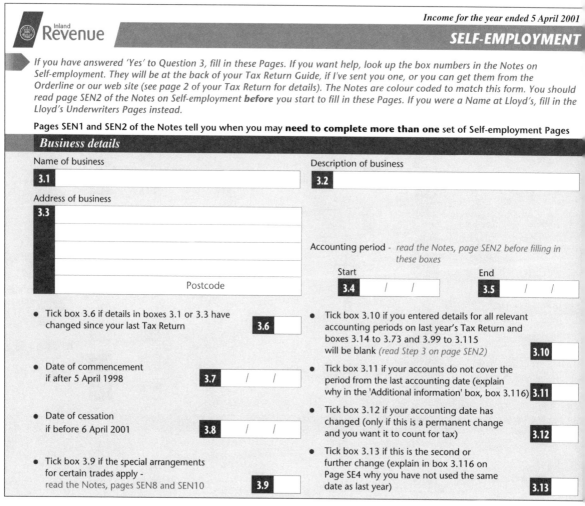

FILL THIS IN IF:

You had income from work done on a self-employed or freelance basis, or you let furnished rooms and provided services so that it was considered as a 'trade'. Do not fill in this form if you were trading as a partnership (see introduction above).

What to enter

State the kind of work you do and your business name and address (it may be your normal name or a trading name) and fill in boxes 3.4 and 3.5 with the relevant dates.

Boxes 3.10 to 3.13 need ticking where relevant – they are designed to let the tax office know of any change in your business accounting dates. Fill in box 3.7 if you have started in business since 5 April 1998, and fill in 3.8 if you have ceased trading before 6 April 2001.

Capital allowances - summary

	Capital allowances	Balancing charge
Motor cars (Separate calculations must be made for each motor car costing more than £12,000 and for cars used partly for private motoring.)	**3.14** £	**3.15** £
Other business plant and machinery	**3.16** £	**3.17** £
Agricultural or Industrial Buildings Allowance (A separate calculation must be made for each block of expenditure.)	**3.18** £	**3.19** £
Other capital allowances claimed (Separate calculations must be made.)	**3.20** £	**3.21** £
Total capital allowances/balancing charges	total of column above **3.22** £	total of column above **3.23** £

What to enter

Any depreciation shown in your accounts will have been added back as disallowable in assessing your profit for tax purposes (see page 39); instead you can claim capital allowances as set out in the table below. (A balancing charge arises if you sell an asset for more than its tax written down value – that is its original cost less cumulative capital allowances claimed.)

FILL THIS IN IF:

You wish to claim capital allowances – regardless of your turnover level.

Table of capital allowances	First year capital allowance	Writing down % on reducing balance thereafter
	From 2 July 1998	
	%	%
Plant, machinery and equipment*	40†	25
Fixtures and fittings	40†	25
Motor cars (maximum £3,000 a year)	–	25
Vans and lorries	40†	25
Office furniture and equipment	40†	25
Insulation of factories and warehouses	40†	25
Fire safety expenditure	40†	25
	From 1 April 2000	
Computer hardware and software, high tech mobile phones and internet set-top boxes	to 31 March 2003	–
(For small businesses only)‡	100	
		on cost
Factories and warehouses	–	4
Agricultural buildings	–	4
Hotel buildings	–	4
Houses under assured tenancies scheme	–	4

* The annual rate of writing down allowance will be reduced to 6 per cent for most assets with a working life of 25 years or more purchased, or contracted, on or after 26 November 1996, but this applies only to businesses which spend more than £100,000 a year on such assets. This 6 per cent was increased to 12 per cent for purchases during the year ended 1 July 1998 by small or medium-sized companies.
† Only applies to small or medium-sized businesses (see below). There are higher rates for Northern Ireland.
‡ Small businesses are defined as having an annual turnover of not more than £2.8 million, assets not exceeding £1.4 million with a maximum of 50 employees. (The figures for medium-sized businesses are £11.2 million, £5.6 million and 250 employees respectively.)
Notes: There are higher allowances for buildings in enterprise zones, scientific research and film production expenditure, and special provisions for patent rights, know how, mines, mineral rights and certain other assets.
The 25% writing down percentage on the reducing balance means effectively that about 90% of the asset is written off after eight years.

Income and expenses - annual turnover below £15,000

*If your annual turnover is £15,000 or more, **ignore** boxes 3.24 to 3.26. Instead fill in Page SE2*

*If your annual turnover is below £15,000, **fill in boxes 3.24 to 3.26 instead of Page SE2**. Read the Notes, page SEN2.*

- Turnover, other business receipts and goods etc. taken for personal use (and balancing charges from box 3.23) — **3.24** £
- Expenses allowable for tax (including capital allowances from box 3.22) — **3.25** £

Net profit (put figure in brackets if a loss) — box 3.24 *minus* box 3.25 — **3.26** £

What to enter

You only need to give three figures: your turnover, allowable expenses and profit (or loss). Obviously you will have prepared your own accounts in order to obtain these figures.

It is not necessary to send your accounts to the tax office with your tax return but you must keep them so that you can answer any queries that they may raise.

FILL THIS IN IF:

Your business turnover is less than £15,000 a year.

DO NOT FILL THIS IN IF:

Your miscellaneous income from self-employment is from a one-off freelance or spare time activity. You have to declare this income under Miscellaneous Income (see page 15 of this book).

Having filled in this section, now turn to box 3.74 (page 40 in this book), or if your turnover is **more** than £15,000 fill in the following sections.

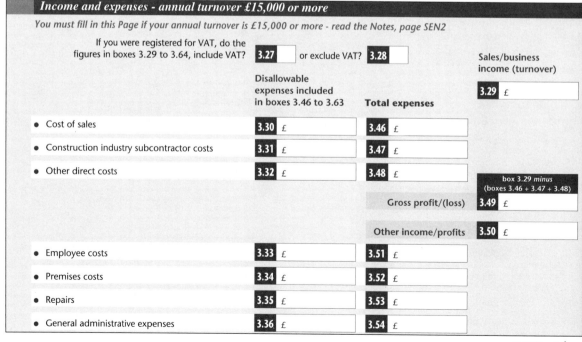

Income and expenses - annual turnover £15,000 or more

You must fill in this Page if your annual turnover is £15,000 or more - read the Notes, page SEN2

If you were registered for VAT, do the figures in boxes 3.29 to 3.64, include VAT? **3.27** or exclude VAT? **3.28**

Sales/business income (turnover)

	Disallowable expenses included in boxes 3.46 to 3.63	Total expenses	
			3.29 £
Cost of sales	**3.30** £	**3.46** £	
Construction industry subcontractor costs	**3.31** £	**3.47** £	
Other direct costs	**3.32** £	**3.48** £	
		Gross profit/(loss)	box 3.29 *minus* (boxes 3.46 + 3.47 + 3.48) **3.49** £
		Other income/profits	**3.50** £
Employee costs	**3.33** £	**3.51** £	
Premises costs	**3.34** £	**3.52** £	
Repairs	**3.35** £	**3.53** £	
General administrative expenses	**3.36** £	**3.54** £	

continued …

• Motor expenses	**3.37** £		**3.55** £	
• Travel and subsistence	**3.38** £		**3.56** £	
• Advertising, promotion and entertainment	**3.39** £		**3.57** £	
• Legal and professional costs	**3.40** £		**3.58** £	
• Bad debts	**3.41** £		**3.59** £	
• Interest	**3.42** £		**3.60** £	
• Other finance charges	**3.43** £		**3.61** £	
• Depreciation and loss/(profit) on sale	**3.44** £		**3.62** £	
• Other expenses	**3.45** £		**3.63** £	

Put the total of boxes 3.30 to 3.45 in **box 3.66 below**

	total of boxes 3.51 to 3.63
Total expenses	**3.64** £

	boxes 3.49 + 3.50 *minus* 3.64
Net profit/(loss)	**3.65** £

FILL THIS IN IF:

Your business turnover is *more* than £15,000 a year.
  (See also boxes 3.27 to 3.54 on the previous page.)

WHERE TO FIND THE INFORMATION

Your financial accounts and records should provide these figures.

What to enter

Not all the expenditure shown in your financial accounts will be allowable for tax against profits, which is why there are two columns of figures – the left-hand column (3.30 to 3.45) identifying any amounts that are disallowable; the figures to go in the right-hand column (3.46 to 3.63) are those shown in your accounts.

Tax adjustments to net profit or loss

	boxes 3.30 to 3.45	
• Disallowable expenses	**3.66** £	
• Goods etc. taken for personal use and other adjustments (apart from disallowable expenses) that increase profits	**3.67** £	
• Balancing charges (from box 3.23)	**3.68** £	
		boxes 3.66 + 3.67 + 3.68
Total additions to net profit (deduct from net loss)		**3.69** £
• Capital allowances (from box 3.22)	**3.70** £	
		boxes 3.70 + 3.71
• Deductions from net profit (add to net loss)	**3.71** £	**3.72** £
		boxes 3.65 + 3.69 *minus* 3.72
Net business profit for tax purposes (put figure in brackets if a loss)		**3.73** £

FILL THIS IN IF:

Your turnover is *above* £15,000 a year and you have completed boxes 3.27 to 3.65.

What to enter

The total disallowable expenses (box 3.66) shown above; an estimate of goods, etc. used personally (box 3.67). Box 3.68 is for any balancing charge (see page 37); Box 3.70 totals your capital allowances (see page 37); Box 3.71 is for any amounts included in your accounts which are either not taxable or not relevant to your business e.g. bank interest earned on your business account although it is more likely that you will have covered these in the disallowable items on the previous page. Complete the remaining boxes.

Adjustments to arrive at taxable profit or loss

Basis period begins **3.74** [/ /] and ends **3.75** [/ /]

Profit or loss of this account for tax purposes (box 3.26 or 3.73) **3.76** £

Adjustment to arrive at profit or loss for this basis period **3.77** £

- Overlap profit brought forward **3.78** £
- Deduct overlap relief used this year **3.79** £

- Overlap profit carried forward **3.80** £

Adjustment for farmers' averaging (see Notes, page SEN8 if you made a loss for 2000-2001) **3.81** £

Adjustment on change of basis **3.82** £

Net profit for 2000-2001 (if loss, enter '0') **3.83** £

Allowable loss for 2000-2001 (if you made a profit, enter '0') **3.84** £

- Loss offset against other income for 2000-2001 **3.85** £
- Loss to carry back **3.86** £
- Loss to carry forward
  (that is allowable loss not claimed in any other way) **3.87** £
- Losses brought forward from earlier years **3.88** £
- Losses brought forward from earlier years used this year **3.89** £

Taxable profit after losses brought forward | box 3.83 *minus* box 3.89 **3.90** £

- Any other business income (for example, Business Start-up Allowance received in 2000-2001) **3.91** £

Total taxable profits from this business | box 3.90 + box 3.91 **3.92** £

- Tick box 3.93 if the figure in box 3.92 is provisional **3.93**

FILL THIS IN IF:

You have completed any of the sections of these supplementary pages so far.

What to enter

The totals (where applicable) from boxes completed on previous pages. (Ask for help sheet IR222 from your tax office.)

REMEMBER:

As well as coping with keeping account books and records and the tax implications generally, self-employed people must understand how the National Insurance system works, otherwise you could have arrears of debt to pay, or find yourself unable to claim certain exemptions or benefits. There is an Inland Revenue helpline for new self-employed people – 0845 915 4515.

Note also that there are special tax rules governing new businesses and those that have ceased trading.

Class 4 National Insurance Contributions

- Tick box 3.94 if exception or deferment applies   **3.94** ▢

- Adjustments to profit chargeable to Class 4 National Insurance Contributions   **3.95** £

Class 4 National Insurance Contributions due   **3.96** £

FILL THIS IN IF:

You are claiming exemption or deferment from Class 4 NIC's; or you have a 'cash basis' adjustment or trading losses brought forward. These NI payments are based on 6% of your taxable profit (after deducting capital allowances, but including any enterprise allowance received) between £4,385 and £27,820.

What to enter

Tick box 3.94 if you are exempted from Class 4 NICs and write in any adjustment in box 3.95.

TAX TIP:

Reasons for exemption or deferment may be due to your age, profit levels or infirmity. Ask for leaflet CA72.

Subcontractors in the construction industry

- Deductions made by contractors on account of tax (you must send your CIS25s to us)   **3.97** £

FILL THIS IN IF:

You are a subcontractor in the construction industry and have received any payments under that industry's tax deduction scheme.

What to enter

The amounts shown on form CIS25 which should be sent in with your tax return.

Tax deducted from trading income

- Any tax deducted (excluding deductions made by contractors on account of tax) from trading income.   **3.98** £

FILL THIS IN IF:

Any tax has been deducted from your trading income.

Summary of balance sheet

▶ *Leave these boxes blank if you do not have a balance sheet*

FILL THIS IN IF:

Your turnover is over £15,000 and you are submitting a balance sheet with your profit and loss account.

What to enter

The figures, suitably grouped, from your accounts.

Note: The balance sheet boxes are not shown here – they extend to 3.116.

PARTNERSHIPS

There are two types of partnership tax return – the short version and the long version. Most partnerships will use the short version as their only partnership income will be trading income or taxed income from banks, building societies or deposit takers. All partners are jointly responsible for completing this tax return.

Inland Revenue

Income for the year ended 5 April 2001

PARTNERSHIP (SHORT)

Partnership details

Partnership reference number

4.1

Partnership trade or profession

4.2

- Date you started being a partner (if during 2000-2001) **4.3** / /
- Date you stopped being a partner (if during 2000-2001) **4.4** / /

Your share of the partnership's trading or professional income

Basis period begins **4.5** / /   and ends **4.6** / /

- Your share of the profit or loss of this year's account for tax purposes **4.7** £
- Adjustment to arrive at profit or loss for this basis period **4.8** £
- Overlap profit brought forward **4.9** £   Deduct overlap relief used this year **4.10** £
- Overlap profit carried forward **4.11** £
- Adjustment for farmers' averaging (see Notes, page PN3 if the partnership made a loss in 2000-2001) or foreign tax deducted, if tax credit relief not claimed **4.12** £
- Adjustment on change of basis **4.12A** £

Net profit for 2000-2001 (if loss, enter '0' in box 4.13 and enter the loss in box 4.14) **4.13** £

Allowable loss for 2000-2001 **4.14** £

- Loss offset against other income for 2000-2001 **4.15** £
- Loss to carry back **4.16** £
- Loss to carry forward (that is, allowable loss not claimed in any other way) **4.17** £
- Losses brought forward from last year **4.18** £
- Losses brought forward from last year used this year **4.19** £

Taxable profit after losses brought forward

box 4.13 *minus* box 4.19
4.20 £

- Add amounts **not** included in the partnership accounts that are needed to calculate your taxable profit (for example, Enterprise Allowance (Business Start-up Allowance) received in 2000-2001) **4.21** £

Total taxable profits from this business

box 2.20 + box 2.21
4.22 £

REMEMBER:

All records used to complete the 2000–2001 tax return must be kept until at least 31 January 2007 in case the Inland Revenue wishes to see them.

Class 4 National Insurance Contributions

- Tick this box if exception or deferment applies | **4.23** [ ]
- Adjustments to profit chargeable to Class 4 National Insurance Contributions | **4.24** £

Class 4 National Insurance Contributions due | **4.25** £

Your share of the Partnership taxed income

- Share of taxed income (liable at 20%) | **4.70** £

Your share of Partnership Trading and Professional Profits

from box 4.22

- Share of partnership profits (other than that liable at 20%) | **4.73** £

Your share of the Partnership's tax paid

- Share of Income Tax deducted from Partnership income | **4.74** £
- Share of CIS25 deductions | **4.75** £
- Share of tax deducted from trading income (not CIS25 deductions) | **4.75A** £

boxes 4.74 + 4.75 + 4.75A

4.77 £

4.79 *Additional information*

FILL THIS IN IF:	WHERE TO FIND THE INFORMATION	**What to enter**
You were entitled to a share of profits, losses or income from a business which you carried on in partnership. (See also boxes 4.1 to 4.22 on the previous page.)	You will have received a partnership statement for each partnership for which you were a partner and for each business if the partnership carried on more than one business.	You need to complete separate partnership pages for each business. Some of the information requested is similar to that covered under the self-employed section (see page 36).

LAND AND PROPERTY

Income for the year ended 5 April 2001

Inland Revenue

LAND AND PROPERTY

Fill in these boxes first

Name

Tax reference

If you want help, look up the box numbers in the Notes

Are you claiming Rent a Room relief for gross rents of £4,250 or less?
(Or £2,125 if the claim is shared?)
Read the Notes on page LN2 to find out
- **whether you can claim Rent a Room relief; and**
- **how to claim relief for gross rents over £4,250**

No   Yes

If 'Yes', and this is your only income from UK property, you have finished these Pages

FILL THIS IN IF:

You wish to claim Rent-a-Room relief and the gross rents are £4,250 or less a year. (If more see page 46.)

What to enter

Tick either the 'Yes' or 'No' box; if 'Yes' and you have no other income from land or property you need not complete the rest of this form.

Is your income from furnished holiday lettings?
If 'No', turn over and fill in Page L2 to give details of your property income

No   Yes

If 'Yes', fill in boxes 5.1 to 5.18 before completing Page L2

Furnished holiday lettings

- Income from furnished holiday lettings — **5.1** £

- *Expenses* (furnished holiday lettings only)

- Rent, rates, insurance, ground rents etc. — **5.2** £
- Repairs, maintenance and renewals — **5.3** £
- Finance charges, including interest — **5.4** £
- Legal and professional costs — **5.5** £
- Costs of services provided, including wages — **5.6** £
- Other expenses — **5.7** £

total of boxes 5.2 to 5.7
5.8 £

box 5.1 *minus* box 5.8
5.9 £

Net profit (put figures in brackets if a loss)

- *Tax adjustments*

- Private use — **5.10** £
- Balancing charges — **5.11** £
- Capital allowances — **5.13** £

box 5.10 + box 5.11
5.12 £

boxes 5.9 + 5.12 *minus* box 5.13
5.14 £

Profit for the year (copy to box 5.19). If loss, enter '0' in box 5.14 and put the loss in box 5.15

	boxes 5.9 + 5.12 *minus* box 5.13
Loss for the year (if you have entered '0' in box 5.14)	**5.15** £

■ *Losses*

● Loss offset against 2000-2001 total income	**5.16** £
	see Notes, page LN4
● Loss carried back	**5.17** £
	see Notes, page LN4
● Loss offset against other income from property (copy to box 5.38)	**5.18** £

WHERE TO FIND THE INFORMATION

Records of rent received and expenses paid.

FILL THIS IN IF:

You have income from furnished holiday lettings in the UK (tick the 'Yes' box). Note: the forms start on page 44. Any income from overseas should not be entered here but under the Foreign supplementary pages (see page 47).

What to enter

The relevant income and expenditure. See page 46 for the types of expenditure you can claim and see page 37 for capital allowance details.

Other property income

■ *Income*

	copy from box 5.14	Tax deducted	
● Furnished holiday lettings profits	**5.19** £		
● Rents and other income from land and property	**5.20** £	**5.21** £	
● Chargeable premiums	**5.22** £		boxes 5.19 + 5.20 + 5.22 + 5.22A
● Reverse premiums	**5.22A** £		**5.23** £

■ *Expenses* (do not include figures you have already put in boxes 5.2 to 5.7 on Page L1)

● Rent, rates, insurance, ground rents etc.	**5.24** £	
● Repairs, maintenance and renewals	**5.25** £	
● Finance charges, including interest	**5.26** £	
● Legal and professional costs	**5.27** £	
● Costs of services provided, including wages	**5.28** £	total for boxes 5.24 to 5.29
● Other expenses	**5.29** £	**5.30** £

	box 5.23 *minus* box 5.30
Net profit (put figures in brackets if a loss)	**5.31** £

■ *Tax adjustments*

● Private use	**5.32** £	box 5.32 + box 5.33
● Balancing charges	**5.33** £	**5.34** £
● Rent a Room exempt amount	**5.35** £	
● Capital allowances	**5.36** £	
● 10% wear and tear	**5.37** £	boxes 5.35 to box 5.38
● Furnished holiday lettings losses (from box 5.18)	**5.38** £	**5.39** £

		boxes 5.31 + 5.34 *minus* box 5.39
Adjusted profit (if loss enter '0' in box 5.40 and put the loss in box 5.41)		**5.40** £
	boxes 5.31 + 5.34 *minus* box 5.39	
Adjusted loss (if you have entered '0' in box 5.40)	**5.41** £	
● Loss brought forward from previous year		**5.42** £
		box 5.40 *minus* box 5.42
Profit for the year		**5.43** £

■ *Losses etc*

● Loss offset against total income (read the note on page LN8)	**5.44** £
● Loss to carry forward to following year	**5.45** £
● Pooled expenses from 'one-estate election' carried forward	**5.46** £
● Tick box 5.47 if these Pages include details of property let jointly	**5.47**
● Tick box 5.48 if **all** property income ceased in the year to 5 April 2001 **and** you don't expect to receive such income again, in the year to 5 April 2002	**5.48**

What to enter

The relevant income, expenditure and losses. See below for expenditure you can claim, and see page 37 for capital allowances details.

FILL THIS IN IF:

You have other property or Rent-a-Room income over £4,250 a year.

WHERE TO FIND THE INFORMATION

Records of rent received and expenses paid.

REMEMBER:

Rent-a-Room scheme with income over £4,250 a year:

You have the option of either paying tax on the excess over £4,250 without any deduction for allowable expenses, or calculating any total profit made (gross rents less actual allowable expenses) and paying tax on that profit in the normal way.

An individual's £4,250 limit is halved if, at any time during a tax year, someone else received income from letting the same property.

JOINT NAMES

If a *husband and wife* own a property that is let, the tax office will assume that any income from this asset is divided equally. You should enter in your tax return one half of the income and expenses, and tick box 5.47 to indicate to the tax office that it is a joint holding.

If the ownership is *not* held equally, then ask your tax office for form 17 in which you can jointly declare the actual ownership split. Such declaration takes effect from the date it is made provided that the form is sent to your tax office within 60 days.

TAX TIP:

What expenses can you claim against property income?

Some or all of the following should be considered:

Rent paid, business and water rates

General maintenance and repairs of the property, garden, furniture and fittings

Costs of agents for letting and collecting rents

Insurance

Interest payable on a loan to purchase or improve investment property

Charges for preparing inventories

Legal fees – on renewing a tenancy agreement, for leases of not more than 50 years, or on the initial grant of a lease not exceeding 21 years

Accountancy fees to prepare and agree your income

Costs of collecting rents, which could in some cases include your travelling expenses to and from the property

Costs of services e.g. porters, cleaners, security

Wear and tear allowance for furniture and fittings – generally 10 per cent of the basic rent receivable. As an alternative, the cost of renewals may be claimed

Council tax

FOREIGN

You will need these forms if you receive income, pensions, social security benefits, etc. from abroad.

Income and gains and tax credit relief for the year ended 5 April 2001

 Inland Revenue

FOREIGN

Name	Tax reference

Fill in these boxes first

If you want help, look up the box numbers in the Notes

Foreign savings

Fill in columns A to E, and tick the box in column E if you want to claim tax credit relief.

Country A (tick box if income is unremittable) ▼	Amount before tax B	UK tax C	Foreign tax D	Amount chargeable E (tick box to claim tax credit relief) ▼
■ *Interest, and other income from overseas savings* -see Notes, page FN4	£	£	£	£
	£	£	£	£
	£	£	£	£

FILL THIS IN IF:	WHERE TO FIND THE INFORMATION
You receive income, pensions or benefits from abroad.	Overseas dividend vouchers, bank statements, overseas pension and social security benefit statements, foreign tax assessments and actual receipts for any foreign tax paid.

What to enter

These supplementary pages are divided into four sections. Only the first part of the form is reproduced above.

Boxes 6.1 and 6.2A cover income from foreign savings – fill in the figures in the appropriate columns.

Boxes 6.3 to 6.8 are for other overseas income, including pensions and social security benefits.

Boxes 6.9 and 6.10 enable you to reclaim any foreign tax paid.

Boxes 6.11 to 6.38 cover income from land and property abroad – the information required is similar to that for income from UK land and property (see page 44).

REMEMBER:

Keep details as to how you make up the figures for although you do not have to enter the names and addresses of the properties, pension providers, etc. on the form, the tax office may ask for them.

Capital gains should be shown on the Capital Gains pages (see page 49) not on these Foreign pages.

TRUSTS, SETTLEMENTS AND ESTATES

You will need this form if you received income from a trust, settlement or estate.

Income for the year ended 5 April 2001

Inland Revenue

TRUSTS ETC.

Income from trusts and settlements

■ *Income taxed at:*

	Income receivable	Tax paid	Taxable amount
● 'rate applicable to trusts'	7.1 £	7.2 £	7.3 £
● basic rate	7.4 £	7.5 £	7.6 £
● the lower rate	7.7 £	7.8 £	7.9 £
● the dividend rate	7.10 £	7.11 £	7.12 £

FILL THIS IN IF:

You were entitled to receive income from a trust fund set up by someone else or you have income from a discretionary or accumulation trust.

WHERE TO FIND THE INFORMATION

You should receive a statement or certificate from the trustees – ask for one if you have not received it.

What to enter

Fill in the boxes showing income received, tax paid and gross amount (i.e. taxable amount) differentiating between the various tax rates.

Income from the estates of deceased persons

■ *Income bearing:*

	Income receivable	Tax paid	Taxable amount
● basic rate tax	7.13 £	7.14 £	7.15 £
● lower rate tax	7.16 £	7.17 £	7.18 £
● repayable dividend rate	7.19 £	7.20 £	7.21 £
● non-repayable basic rate tax	7.22 £	7.23 £	7.24 £
● non-repayable lower rate tax	7.25 £	7.26 £	7.27 £
● non-repayable dividend rate	7.28 £	7.29 £	7.30 £
● total foreign tax for which tax credit relief not claimed	7.31 £		

FILL THIS IN IF:

You have received any payment from the estate of someone who has died.

WHERE TO FIND THE INFORMATION

The personal representative or solicitor should send you a statement giving details and a tax deduction certificate (form RI85) showing the tax that has been deducted.

What to enter

As with trusts above, complete the boxes differentiating between the various tax rates.

CAPITAL GAINS

A capital gain is any profit arising when you sell, transfer, give, receive compensation for, or otherwise dispose of any of your assets or possessions.

Some assets are exempt from this tax (see page 50) but you may need to fill in these pages if you have made a capital profit (or loss) on assets that are taxable.

You do not pay tax on the price you receive for the asset, but only on the increase in its value whilst you have owned it, after relief for inflation.

for the year ended 5 April 2001

 Inland **Revenue**

 **CAPITAL GAINS**

FILL THIS IN IF:

You sold or gave away assets to the value of £14,400 or more and your chargeable gains for tax purposes were £7,200 or more in the year ended 5 April 2001.

WHERE TO FIND THE INFORMATION

You will need copies of contract notes for the sale or purchase of shares; invoices and letters about the purchase or sale of other assets, and invoices for allowable expenses which you can claim.

What to enter

The first three pages of the capital gains forms enable you to detail the relevant assets and then total them in boxes 8.1 to 8.6 (not shown above).

These are then summarised in boxes Q, U, L and O and 8.7 to 8.21 so as to record any gain or loss and any carried forward figures.

The tax rates and exemption limits are shown on page 69.

REMEMBER:

There is relief for inflation – a combination of an indexation allowance and tapering relief. A higher rate of relief is available for business assets. The percentages and formulae used will be detailed in the notes that come from your tax office with this form.

Chargeable gains and allowable losses

Once you have completed Page CG1, or Pages CG2 to CG6, fill in this Page.

Have you 'ticked' any row in Column B, 'Tick box if estimate or valuation used' on Pages CG1 or CG2?	*NO*	*YES*
Have you given details in Column G on Pages CG2 and CG3 of any Capital Gains reliefs claimed or due?	*NO*	*YES*
Are you claiming, and/or using, any 'clogged' losses (see Notes, page CGN10)?	*NO*	*YES*

Enter the number of transactions from Page CG1 or column AA on Page CG2 for:

- transactions in quoted shares or other securities — box Q

- transactions in other shares or securities — box U

- transactions in land and property — box L

- other transactions — box O

Total taxable gains (from Page CG1 **or** Page CG3)	**8.7** £	
Your taxable gains *minus* the annual exempt amount of £7,200 (leave blank if '0' or negative)	box 8.7 minus £7,200 **8.8** £	
Additional liability in respect of non-resident or dual resident trusts (see Notes, page CGN6)	**8.9** £	

Capital losses

(Remember if your loss arose on a transaction with a connected person, see Notes page CGN13, you can only set that loss against gains you make on disposals to that same connected person.)

■ *This year's losses*

- Total (from box 8.2 on Page CG3 or box F2 on Page CG1) — **8.10** £

- Used against gains (total of column K1 on Page CG3, or the smaller of boxes F1 and F2 on Page CG1) — **8.11** £

- Used against earlier years' gains (generally only available to personal representatives, see Notes, page CGN11) — **8.12** £

- Used against income (only losses of the type described on page CGN9 can be used against income) — **8.13A** £ amount claimed against income of 2000-2001; **8.13B** £ amount claimed against income of 1999-2000; box 8.13A + box 8.13B **8.13** £

- This year's unused losses — box 8.10 *minus* (boxes 8.11 + 8.12 + 8.13) **8.14** £

■ *Earlier years' losses*

- Unused losses of 1996-97 and later years — **8.15** £

- Used this year (losses from box 8.15 are used in priority to losses from box 8.18) (column K3 on Page CG3 or box F6 on Page CG1) — **8.16** £

- Remaining unused losses of 1996-97 and later years — box 8.15 *minus* box 8.16 **8.17** £

- Unused losses of 1995-96 and earlier years — **8.18** £

- Used this year (losses from box 8.15 are used in priority to losses from box 8.18) (column K3 on Page CG3 or box F6 on Page CG1) — box 8.6 *minus* box 8.16 (or box F6 *minus* box 8.16) **8.19** £

■ *Total of unused losses to carry forward*

- Carried forward losses of 1996-97 and later years — box 8.14 + box 8.17 **8.20** £

- Carried forward losses of 1995-96 and earlier years — box 8.18 *minus* box 8.19 **8.21** £

Refer to the notes on the previous page.

Assets which are free from capital gains tax

Private motor cars.
A house owned and occupied by you which is your main residence.
Chattels – such as jewellery, pictures and furniture – where the proceeds are £6,000 or less, with marginal relief up to £15,000.
Life policies and deferred annuities (unless sold on by original owner).
National Savings Certificates; Premium Bonds.
Shares subscribed for under the BES and EIS.
Shares subscribed for in approved quoted Venture Capital Trusts.
Personal Equity Plan (PEP) investments.
Individual Savings Accounts (ISAs).
Save As You Earn schemes.

TESSA accounts.
Government stocks and public corporation stocks guaranteed by the Government.
Qualifying corporate bonds.
Gambling, pools and lottery winnings and prizes.
Decorations for gallantry, unless purchased.
Compensation for damages.
Gifts of assets to a charity.
Gifts of outstanding public interest given to the nation.
Land and buildings given to the National Trust
Compensation for mis-sold personal pensions and AVC's between 29-4-88 and 30-6-94.
Foreign currency for personal use.

NON-RESIDENCE

Whether you are resident or domiciled in the UK or abroad can affect your liability to income tax or capital gains tax.

For the year ended 5 April 2001

Inland Revenue

NON-RESIDENCE ETC.

Name	Tax reference

Fill in these boxes first

Residence status

I am *(please tick appropriate box)*

- resident in the UK | 9.1 |
- ordinarily resident in the UK | 9.3 |
- not domiciled in the UK (and it is relevant to my Income Tax or Capital Gains Tax liability) | 9.5 |
- claiming personal allowances as a non-resident | 9.7 |

- not resident in the UK | 9.2 |
- not ordinarily resident in the UK | 9.4 |
- claiming split-year treatment | 9.6 |
- resident in a country other than the UK (under a double taxation agreement) at the same time as being resident in the UK | 9.8 |

Information required if you claim to be non-resident in the UK for the whole of 2000-2001

- Are you in any of the following categories:

  - a Commonwealth citizen (this includes a British citizen) or an EEA (European Economic Area) national?

  - a present or former employee of the British Crown (including a civil servant, member of the armed forces etc)?

  - a UK missionary society employee?

  - a civil servant in a territory under the protection of the British Crown?

  - a resident of the Isle of Man or the Channel Islands?

  - a former resident of the UK and you live abroad for the sake of your own health or the health of a member of your family who lives with you?

  - a widow or widower of an employee of the British Crown?

  Yes | 9.9 | No | 9.10 |

- How many days have you spent in the UK, excluding days of arrival and departure, during the year ended 5 April 2001? *Enter the number of days* | 9.11 | *days*

FILL THIS IN IF:

You know that you are non-resident or domiciled in the UK for tax purposes, or if you have moved abroad or have been living abroad, for this may affect your tax status and tax liabilities (only the first part of the form is reproduced here).

TAX TIP:

The rules governing the legal status of a person and the tax implications are amongst some of the most difficult tax legislation, and it is wise to get a tax adviser to handle these matters for you.

What to enter

These supplementary pages (up to box 9.35) contain a sequence of questions so that the tax office can establish your status for tax purposes.

PAYE Coding Notice

The tax office gives employers a PAYE code for each of their employees. This code is made up from the information your tax office have on their files either as a result of information that they have found out or from a tax return form sent in by you. The tax office send you a Coding Notice similar to that shown below, which you need to check. If it is wrong you will pay the incorrect amount of tax. Your employers are told only the code (not the full details) so that they can calculate how much of your pay is tax free.

Inland **Revenue**

PAYE Coding Notice

This form shows your tax code for the tax year

Please keep all your coding notices. You may need to refer to them if you have to fill in a Tax Return.

Please quote your Tax reference and National Insurance number if you contact us

Tax Office telephone	Date of issue
Tax reference	National Insurance number

Your tax code for the year shown above is

This tax code is used to deduct tax payable on your income from

If you move to another job, your new employer will normally continue to use this tax code.
The tax code is worked out as follows:

See note	Your tax allowances	£
	Total allowances **A**	

The left-hand side shows your allowances, allowable expenses, and any claim for higher-rate tax relief on allowable payments on which basic rate tax has been deducted (e.g. a personal pension payment, or Gift Aid to charity). Payments to personal pension plans and free-standing additional voluntary contribution schemes will also be shown here.

There may also be a note of estimated total income to be used in calculating your age allowance restriction.

The new children's tax credit will also be shown here but the relief is only at 10% so there will be a restriction shown on the right-hand side.

C Your tax free amount for the year is £   , making your tax code

See example overleaf

The right-hand side shows any taxable State Pension or benefits you have received, e.g. a company car, fuel, medical insurance.

Other figures could refer to casual earnings, after expenses, declared by you on your tax return (or an estimate made by the tax office).

Any untaxed interest will be stated here. Any under or over payment of tax will refer to a notice of assessment for a previous year.

Remember that the married couple's allowance, additional personal allowance and relief for maintenance payments were all withdrawn from 6 April 2000 but the married couple's allowance and maintenance relief continues for those couples where either the husband or wife was born before 6 April 1935 (see page 23).

The full amount of these allowances will be shown on the left-hand side, but as the relief is restricted to only 10 per cent then there will be an 'allowance restriction' on the right-hand side; the amount will depend on any age allowance claimed. Tax relief on the children's tax credit is also restricted to 10 per cent, so again there will be a 'restriction'.

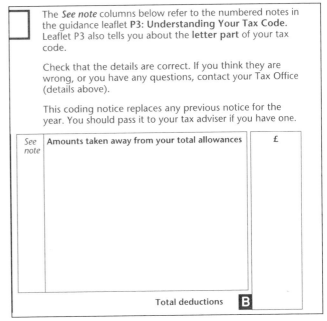

The *See note* columns below refer to the numbered notes in the guidance leaflet **P3: Understanding Your Tax Code.** Leaflet P3 also tells you about the **letter part** of your tax code.

Check that the details are correct. If you think they are wrong, or you have any questions, contact your Tax Office (details above).

This coding notice replaces any previous notice for the year. You should pass it to your tax adviser if you have one.

See note	Amounts taken away from your total allowances	£
	Total deductions **B**	

TAX TIP:

If your coding notice is wrong write to the tax office, or if you haven't filled in a tax return for a year or two then ask for a tax return and fill it in.

Your code is found by deducting the total of the left-hand side from the right-hand side and omitting the last figure. The higher your code, the lower your tax.

What do the letters mean?

The letter shown after your code defines your status. For example, A = basic personal allowance plus 50% of the children's tax credit, and a basic rate taxpayer; (H is used if you are to get all the children's tax credit); L = basic personal allowance; P = full personal allowance if aged 65–74; V being used if you are also entitled to the married couple's allowance and you are on basic rate tax; Y = personal allowance for those aged 75 or over.

OT means that no allowances have been given – that is often used if you haven't sent in a tax return for a long time or your tax affairs are very complicated. Other codes (BR, DO, T and NT) are sometimes used if you are working for more than one employer or have complicated tax affairs.

Sometimes your taxable benefits will exceed your allowances – for example, if you are taxed on car and fuel benefits and private health benefits, or owe back tax. In these cases a K code is used so that your employer can recoup this tax on behalf of the tax office.

Tax repayments

At the end of each tax year you should check to see exactly what income you received during the year and what tax you have actually paid. Use the Quick Tax Check on page 63.

If you have paid too much you can get a repayment of tax. To reclaim tax ask your tax office for form R40. Complete it in the same way as a tax return and send the form to your tax office. You will also find leaflet IR110 very informative.

The forms are available from your tax office by telephoning 0845 9000 404 and there is a new taxback helpline for savers who need to claim a tax repayment – it is 0845 077 6543.

Where most of your income has already had tax deducted before you receive it, you may be able to make quarterly, half-yearly or annual repayment claims.

Is tax being deducted from your savings?

If your total income from all sources for the year does not exceed your allowances and you have any interest from banks, building societies or local authorities, you should register to have such interest paid to you without tax being deducted.

Ask your bank, building society or local authority for form R85, complete it and return it to the branch that holds your account; ask any tax office for booklet IR110 – this has lots of helpful advice and includes form R85 or call the Inland Revenue registration helpline on 0845 980 0645.

Inland Revenue

Savings: application to receive interest without tax taken off

Please read the notes on the back of this form before you start to fill it in.
This form is available in a large print version.

Return this form to your bank, building society or local authority. They will arrange for interest to be paid without tax taken off. They will not acknowledge receipt of the form. You may wish to take a copy for your records.

Joint accounts - each saver must check to see if they can receive their share of the interest without tax taken off and if so complete their own form.

Name of bank, building society or local authority	
Branch	
Account number(s)	

Is this a joint account?   Yes ☐ No ☐
☐ ☐

Details of employee leaving work (form P45)

When you leave an employment, your employer must give you a P45 form. You will get three parts:
Part 1A you keep yourself as a record of your earnings and tax paid, etc.
Parts 2 and 3 you give to your new employer if you start another job. Your new employer will keep part 2, and will complete part 3 and send it to their tax office so that your tax file can be kept up to date and the tax inspector is aware of your movements.

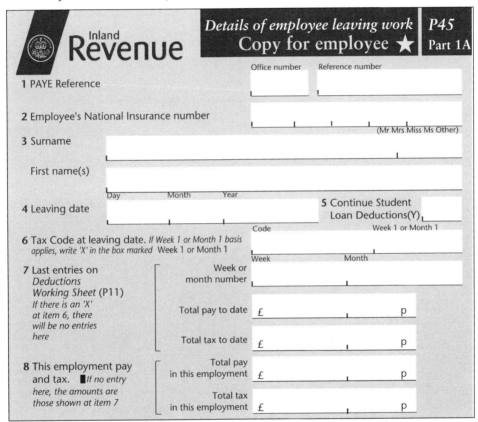

What to do with the form P45

If you have ceased work permanently

Send the form to your tax office whose district is stamped on the form. Also write a letter confirming that you have either retired, ceased working or have become self-employed and ask for a claim form for any tax repayment due.

If you have ceased work temporarily

When you change employment or are made redundant, and there is a gap between one job and the next, send in your form P45 as above, stating that you are temporarily unemployed. Alternatively, if you are claiming the jobseeker's allowance, hand your P45 to your Benefit Office and they will advise you on the proportion of any benefit that is taxable. Normally any adjustments to your tax liability will be made when you start a new employment in the current tax year.
If you do not start a job by the following 5 April, check your total income and tax to see if there is a repayment or underpayment of tax due (use the Quick Guide on page 63).

Certificate of pay, income tax and NIC (form P60)

Your employer has by law to give you a P60 form by 31 May after the end of every tax year. It may have slight variations in design, but it has to contain the following information:

Do not destroy

Employer's name and address

Tax Office name

For employer's use

Your National Insurance number. →

Employee's details

National Insurance number

Sex

"M" if
"F" if F

Surname

First two forenames

Works/payroll no. etc

National Insurance contributions in this employment (Note: LEL = Lower Earnings Limit,

The amounts paid by you and your employer in National Insurance contributions. →

NIC table letter	Earnings at the LEL (where earnings reach or exceed the LEL) (whole £s only)	Earnings above the LEL, up to and incl. the *employee's* Earnings Threshold (whole £s only)	Earnings above the *employee's* Earnings Threshold, up to and incl. the *employer's* Earnings Threshold (whole £s only)	Earnings above the *employer's* Earnings Threshold, up to and incl. the UEL (whole £s only)
	1a £	1b £	1c £	1d £

Employee's contributions are payable on earnings above the employee's 'Earnings Threshold', up to and including the 'Upper Earnir *Employer's contributions* are payable on all earnings above the employer's '**Earnings Threshold**'.

These boxes will have totals for the pay you have received from the employer who has issued you with this form together with the amount of tax deducted. There will also be totals for pay and tax in respect of previous employers for whom you worked in this tax year. →

Certificate by Employer/Paying Office:
This form shows your total pay for Income Tax purposes in this employment for the year. Any overtime, bonus, commission etc, statutory sick pay or statutory maternity pay is included. It also shows, for this employment, total Income Tax and National Insurance contributions deducted (less any refunds), Student Loan deductions made, and Tax Credits paid to you.

Pay and Income Tax details   Pay

In previous employment(s)

In this employment ★

Total for year

Employee's Widows & Orphans/Life Assurance contributions in this employment   ★

Indicates a deduction for this insurance.

REMEMBER:

What to do with the form P60:

Keep it as a record of your earnings for the tax year and the amount of tax deducted.

Use it to fill in your tax return.

Use it as additional proof of income if you arrange a mortgage or a loan.

Use it to check any tax assessment that is sent to you.

P60 End of Year Certificate

Tax Office number and Reference

/

Tax Year to 5 April **2 0 0 1**

Employee's private address

To the employee:
Please keep this certificate in a safe place as you will not be able to get a duplicate. **You will need it if you have to fill in a Tax Return.**
You can also use it to check that your employer is deducting the right rate of National Insurance contributions for you and using your correct National Insurance number.
By law you are required to tell the Tax Office of any income that is not fully taxed, even if you are not sent a Tax Return.   *INLAND REVENUE*

Male, emale

If you change your address, please let your Tax Office know

UEL = Upper Earnings Limit)

Total of employee's and employer's contributions payable	Employee's contributions payable	Scheme Contracted-out number *(For Contracted-out Money Purchase Schemes only)*
1e £ p	**1f** £ p	S
•	•	S
•	•	S
•	•	S

gs Limit'.

£ p	**Tax deducted** £ p	
•	•	Enter "R" in this box if net refund
•	•	
•	•	

Student Loan Deductions in this employment
£

Tax Credits in this employment
£   p

The figures aside marked ★ should be used for your Tax Return, if you get one

£ p	**Final tax code**	Week 53 payment indicator
•		

Your tax reference number and the tax year to which the form relates.

Reference number of contracted-out money purchase pension scheme.

FINANCIAL TIP:

Write to The Benefits Agency, at DSS Longbenton, Benton Park Road, Newcastle upon Tyne, NE98 1YX if you want a written State retirement pension projection.

Your tax code at the year end – this will probably also apply for 2001–2002, so check to see if it is correct (see page 52).

Sometimes the PAYE year has 53 weeks instead of 52. (This box is for the convenience of the tax office.)

Return of expenses and benefits (form P11D)

The form reproduced below is completed annually by an employer for all staff who receive earnings, expenses and benefits which total £8,500 a year or more, and for all directors.
It shows all perks, benefits and expenses that were paid or given by your employer.
Your employers should give you a copy of this form, which they will have sent to the tax office by 6 July, as you need to know what figures to put in your tax return. You also need to have the figures so that you can check any tax assessment sent to you and to check your PAYE code.
Those boxes with 1A on the right-hand side identify those benefits on which the employer (but not the employee) has to pay National Insurance contributions with effect from 6 April 2000.

Inland Revenue

P11D EXPENSES AND BENEFITS 2000-2001

Note to employer
Complete this return for a director, or an employee who earned at a rate of £8,500 a year or more during the year 6 April 2000 to 5 April 2001. Do not include expenses and benefits covered by a dispensation or PAYE settlement agreement. Read the P11D Guide and booklet 480, Chapter 24, before you complete the form. Send the completed P11D and form P11D(b) to the Inland Revenue office by 6 July 2001. You must give a copy of this information to the director or employee by the same date. The term employee is used to cover both directors and employees throughout the rest of this form.

Note to employee
Your employer has filled in this form. Keep it in a safe place as you may not be able to get a duplicate. You will need it for your tax records and to complete your 2000-2001 Tax Return if you get one. Your tax code may need to be adjusted to take account of the information given on this P11D. The box numbers on this P11D have the same numbering as the Employment Pages of the Tax Return, for example, 1.12. Include the total figures in the corresponding box on the Tax Return, unless you think some other figure is more appropriate.

Employer's details
Employer's name

PAYE tax reference

Employee's details
Employee's name

If a director tick here ▶

Works number /department

National Insurance number

From 6 April 2000 employers pay Class 1A National Insurance contributions on more benefits. These are shown in boxes which are brown and have a **1A** indicator

A	**Assets transferred (cars, property, goods or other assets)**	Cost/ Market value	Amount made good or from which tax deducted	Cash equivalent	
	Description of asset	£	– £	= **1.12** £	1A

B	**Payments made on behalf of employee**	
	Description of payment	**1.12** £
	Tax on notional payments not borne by employee within 30 days of receipt of each notional payment	**1.12** £

C	**Vouchers or credit cards**	Gross amount	Amount made good or from which tax deducted	Cash equivalent
	Value of vouchers and payments made using credit cards or tokens	£	– £	= **1.13** £

D	**Living accommodation**	Cash equivalent	
	Cash equivalent of accommodation provided for employee, or his/ her family or household	**1.14** £	1A

E	**Mileage allowance**	Gross amount	Amount made good or from which tax deducted	Taxable payment
	Car and mileage allowances paid for employee's car	£	– £	= **1.15** £

F **Cars and car fuel** *If more than two cars were made available, either at the same time or in succession, please give details on a separate sheet*

	Car 1	Car 2
Make and Model		
Date first registered	/ /	/ /
Dates car was available	From / / to / /	From / / to / /

	2,499 or less	2,500 to 17,999	18,000 or more	2,499 or less	2,500 to 17,999	18,000 or more
Business mileage used in calculation *Tick only one box for each car. If the car was not available for part of the year, the business mileage limits are reduced proportionately.*	☐	☐	☐	☐	☐	☐
	Engine size in cc		Petrol Diesel	Engine size in cc		Petrol Diesel
Enter engine size and tick type of fuel *only if there is a car fuel scale charge*	☐ cc		☐ ☐	☐ cc		☐ ☐
List price of car *If there is no list price, or if it is a classic car, employers see booklet 480; employees see leaflet IR133*	£			£		
Price of optional accessories fitted when car was first made available to the employee	£			£		
Price of accessories added after the car was first made available to the employee	£			£		
Capital contributions (maximum £5,000) the employee made towards the cost of car or accessories	£			£		
Amount paid by employee for private use of the car	£			£		
Cash equivalent of each car	£			£		
Total cash equivalent of all cars available in 2000-2001					**1.16** £	1A
Cash equivalent of fuel for each car	£			£		
Total cash equivalent of fuel for all cars available in 2000-2001					**1.17** £	1A

Car benefit

The annual tax benefit for 2000–2001 is calculated as a percentage of the manufacturer's list price when new (less any personal contribution up to £5,000) – and includes delivery charges, VAT and any accessories over £100 added to the vehicle, unless they were for disabled persons. The percentages are based on the list price and on your annual business mileage as follows:

35% business mileage under 2,500
25% business mileage 2,500 to 17,999
15% business mileage 18,000 and over.

The benefit is reduced by 25% for cars aged four years old and more at the end of the tax year.

There are higher percentages for a second car, and different valuations for classic cars with the list price capped at £80,000.

Fuel benefit

If your employer provides fuel for your private motoring and you do not reimburse the full cost, you will be taxed on this benefit (see table below).

Mileage allowance

If employers pay a mileage allowance to employees who use their own car or bicycle for business, then any payment in excess of the official tax-free mileage rates will be taxable.

Car Mileage Allowance	Up to 4,000 miles		On each mile over 4,000 miles	
	2000–01	2001–02	2000–01	2001–02
Cars up to:				
1,000cc	28p	40p	17p	25p
1,001–1,500cc	35p	40p	20p	25p
1,501–2,000cc	45p	45p	25p	25p
over 2,000cc	63p	63p	36p	36p

Private fuel benefit	2001–2002		2000–2001	
	Petrol £	Diesel £	Petrol £	Diesel £
1,400cc or less	1,930	2,460	1,700	2,170
1,401cc to 2,000cc	2,460	2,460	2,170	2,170
Over 2,000cc	3,620	3,620	3,200	3,200

There is no reduction for high business mileage.

Bicycle mileage allowance is 12p and motorcycle mileage allowance is 24p for both 2000–01 and 2001–02.

G Vans

Cash equivalent of all vans made available for private use | **1.18** £ |

H Interest-free and low interest loans
If the total amount outstanding on all loans does not exceed £5,000 at any time in the year, there is no need for details in this section.

	Loan 1	Loan 2
Number of joint borrowers *(if applicable)*		
Amount outstanding at 5 April 2000 or at date loan was made if later	£	£
Amount outstanding at 5 April 2001 or at date loan was discharged if earlier	£	£
Maximum amount outstanding at any time in the year	£	£
Total amount of interest paid by the borrower in 2000-2001– *enter "NIL" if none was paid*	£	£
Date loan was made in 2000-2001 if applicable	/ /	/ /
Date loan was discharged in 2000-2001 if applicable	/ /	/ /
Cash equivalent of loans after deducting any interest paid by the borrower	**1.19** £ **1A**	**1.19** £

I Private medical treatment or insurance

	Cost to you	Amount made good or from which tax deducted	Cash equivalent
Private medical treatment or insurance	£	– £	= **1.21** £

J Qualifying relocation expenses payments and benefits
Non-qualifying benefits and expenses go in N and O below

Excess over £8,000 of all qualifying relocation expenses payments and benefits for each move | **1.22** £ |

K Services supplied

	Cost to you	Amount made good or from which tax deducted	Cash equivalent
Services supplied to the employee	£	– £	= **1.22** £

L Assets placed at the employee's disposal

	Annual value plus expenses incurred	Amount made good or from which tax deducted	Cash equivalent
Description of asset	£	– £	= **1.22** £

M Shares

Tick the box if during the year there have been share-related benefits for the employee | ☐ |

N Other items (including subscriptions and professional fees)

	Cost to you	Amount made good or from which tax deducted	Cash equivalent
Description of other items	£	– £	= **1.22**
Description of other items	£	– £	= **1.22** £
			Tax paid
Income tax paid but not deducted from director's remuneration			**1.22**

O Expenses payments made to, or on behalf of, the employee

	Cost to you	Amount made good or from which tax deducted	Taxable payment
Travelling and subsistence payments	£	– £	= **1.23** £
Entertainment *(trading organisations read P11D Guide and then enter a tick or a cross as appropriate here)* ☐	£	– £	= **1.23** £
General expenses allowance for business travel	£	– £	= **1.23** £
Payments for use of home telephone	£	– £	= **1.23** £
Non-qualifying relocation expenses *(those not shown in section J)*	£	– £	= **1.23** £
Description of other expenses	£	– £	= **1.23** £

Is your benefit taxable?

Benefit for 2000–2001	Employees earning £8,500 a year or more and directors	Employees earning less than £8,500 a year
Assets provided for your use free of charge (e.g. video)	Taxable at 20% of initial market value	Usually tax free
Canteen facilities available to directors and staff	Not taxable	Not taxable
Car parking facilities at work	Not taxable	Not taxable
Cash vouchers	Taxable	Taxable
Child care facilities (if qualifying conditions met)	Not taxable	Not taxable
Clothing and other goods given to you by your employer	Taxable	Taxed on second-hand value
Company cars, vans, etc.	Taxable at varying rates	Not taxable
Computer equipment provided free	Not taxable on first £2,500 of computer's value	
Credit cards (for personal not business expenditure)	Taxable	Taxable
Exam prizes	Not taxable if reasonable and not part of employment contract	
Fuel for private use	Taxable at scale rate	Not taxable
Holidays	Taxable apart from business element	If employer pays directly, tax free
Interest-free loan	Normally taxable	Not taxable
In-house benefits	Taxable only on the value of the marginal or additional cost to the employer	
Jobfinder's grant	Not taxable	Not taxable
Living accommodation	Normally taxable at annual value unless essential for your employment	
Luncheon vouchers	Tax free up to 15p per working day.	
Mobile telephones provided by employer	Not taxable	Not taxable
Outplacement counselling	Not taxable	Not taxable
Pension contributions and death benefits	Normally tax free	
Private health schemes	Taxable	Not taxable
Prizes and incentive awards	Taxable	Taxable
Relocation expenses (if qualifying)	Tax free up to £8,000	
Scholarships provided by employers' trust	Taxable	Not taxable
Season tickets for travel paid directly by employer	Taxable	Taxable
Share incentive schemes approved by tax inspector	Not taxable	Not taxable
Sick pay schemes	Taxable	Taxable
Workplace sports facilities	Not taxable	Not taxable

How to calculate your own tax

The tax system in the UK is unnecessarily complicated and gets worse year by year as the annual budget statements pile on even more regulations, new types of taxes and tax credits, and endless tinkering with allowances you can (or cannot) claim.

Do I have to calculate my own tax?
No, you do not have to calculate your own tax at all if you do not want to, but if you do not, how will you ever know if you are paying the correct amount of tax? How will you know if your PAYE code number is correct? How will you know if you should be paying some tax on account during the year, or indeed, claiming a refund?

What do I say to the tax office?
When you complete your tax return, Q18 (see page 25 in this book) asks whether you want to calculate your own tax. If you say 'No' and you send your tax return in before 30 September or two months after the date the return form was sent to you, if later, the tax office will do it for you. If you send in your return after that date, the tax office will still calculate any tax due (or overpaid), but they will not guarantee to do it before 31 January and if you haven't paid enough you will have to pay interest on that amount.

If you tick the 'Yes' box in Q18 then you can, if you want to, use the Tax Calculation Guide (SA151W) that will have been sent to you with your tax return.

I don't have a copy of this guide
If the Tax Calculation Guide does not come with your tax return, telephone 0845 9000 404 – this is the Inland Revenue order line – and they will send you a copy and indeed any other form you may request.

What do all the box numbers mean?
All the boxes are numbered according to those in your main tax return plus any supplementary pages that apply to your circumstances, and although these forms look frighteningly complicated it is really a question of transferring all the figures into the correct summary boxes and following the instructions to ensure that you do the additions and subtractions according to the right sequence.

If you have capital gains, you will need supplementary sheets (see page 49) and the notes that come with them have additional calculation boxes.

Is there an easier way of checking my tax?
The Tax Calculation Guide that comes with your tax return is difficult to use because it has to cater for every conceivable contingency. In fact, most people will not need to use many of the boxes at all.

If you tax affairs are not too complicated you may find it useful to use the quick tax check reproduced on the next two pages.

A quick tax check

This quick tax check will be useful for the majority of taxpayers, but will not cover *every* conceivable variation.

The layout is designed for the year ended 5 April 2001 but you could use it for earlier years provided you alter the tax rates and include those allowances that have since ceased (refer to page 69).

Do not include any income that is tax free (e.g. PEPs, TESSAs, ISAs, the first £70 interest on National Savings ordinary accounts or National Savings Certificate interest).

	Tax deducted	Gross amount
Your non-savings income		
Salary or wages, including profit-sharing schemes, but after deducting any pension scheme contribution, payroll giving or tax-free profit-related pay	....	....
State pension		....
Other pensions	....	....
Benefits from employer (see P11D form)		....
Profits from self-employment (usually the accounts period ending in the 2000–2001 tax year) or freelance earnings, after capital allowances and loss relief		....
Casual earnings, after expenses		....
Social Security benefits that are taxable		....
Income from land and property, after expenses (exclude tax-free rental under Rent-a-Room scheme)		....
Total non-savings income	(a) £....................	(A) £....................
Less: allowable expenses		
Personal pension contributions, including retirement annuity contribution for this year (exclude any carry back to previous year and contributions deducted from salary under PAYE above)	....	....
Charitable covenant or gift aid donations	....	....
Interest paid on qualifying loans	....	....
Other expenses allowed for tax	....	....
Total allowable expenses	(b) £....................	(B) £....................
Savings income (excl. dividends)		
Interest received	....	....
Dividend income		
Dividends received (you should add the tax credit to this and then show it separately in the tax deducted column)	....	....
Total savings and dividend income	(c) £....................	(C) £....................
Total income and tax deducted	a–b+c=(d) £....................	(D) £....................
		A–B+C=D

Less: Allowances claim

Personal allowance/age allowance (but deduct
any income limit reduction if over 65 – see
table on page 69) ....

Blind person's allowance ....

<u>Income on which tax is payable</u> (D minus total allowances)   (E) £ ....

Tax payable (see band limits on page 69 and notes below)

First £1,520 of income at 10% ....

Non-savings income

£   at 22% ....

£   at 40% ....

Savings income

£   at 20% ....

£   at 40% ....

Dividend income

£   at 10% ....

£   at 32.5% ....

(E) £ _____   Total (F) £ _____

less: Your claim for personal allowances that are available at only 10%

Married couple's allowance ....

Maintenance or alimony (max £2,000) ....

     (G) £ .... at 10% = (H) £ ....

     (F–H=I) £ ....

less: Enterprise Investment Scheme or
Venture Capital Trust £   at 20% ....

     (J) £ ....

less: Tax already deducted   (d) £ ....

Tax due (or refundable if this is a minus figure)   £ ....

Note: You cannot reclaim the 10 per cent tax credit on dividends.

You will need to add to this sum Class 4 National Insurance liability, any Capital Gains liability and any underpayment from a previous year (or deduct any tax repayment received).

Allocation of tax rate bands

You are taxed at 10 per cent of your first £1,520 of taxable income, whatever its source.
Then you pay 22 per cent on the next £26,880 of earned or pension income, or 20 per cent of savings income, and 10 per cent on dividend income if you are not a higher-rate taxpayer. After that, you pay 40 per cent on everything except dividend income which is charged at 32.5 per cent.

Reference notes

Keep notes throughout the year of all changes in your circumstances, your income and expenses, investments and savings so you have everything to hand when you come to fill in your tax return.

Employment income

Other income

Expenses notes

Pension scheme information

Company car details and other benefits

Savings accounts

PEP details

TESSA details

ISA details

Investment notes

Dividends, interest, etc.

Payroll giving schemes and gift aid amounts

Deeds of covenant

House and mortgage data

Gifts received

Family matters (children's income, etc.)

Insurance matters (check values every year)

Home and contents ❑   Personal belongings ❑   Life ❑   Accident, etc. ❑

General reminders

REMEMBER:

With self assessment tax legislation, the law requires you to keep all records of earnings, income, benefits, profits, expenses, etc. and all other relevant information for 22 months from the end of the tax year if you are employed, and for 5 years and 10 months if you are self-employed.

Personal reminders

National Insurance number ....

Tax reference number ....

Tax office address ....

....

....

Tax returns	Date sent to tax office	Date agreed with Inland Revenue
1999	....	....
2000	....	....
2001	....	....

	1999–2000	2000–2001	2001–2002
PAYE code checked	☐	☐	☐
P60 form from employer checked	☐	☐	☐

Notes on correspondence:

....
....
....
....
....
....
....
....
....

If you leave it to the last minute, you could run out of time

Rates of tax and allowances

Income tax	2001–2002	2000–2001	1999–2000
Starting rate at 10%	£1,880	£1,520	£1,500
Basic rate at 22%†	£1,881–£29,400	£1,521–£28,400	–
Basic rate at 23%†	–	–	£1,501–£28,000
Higher rate at 40%	over £29,400	over £28,400	over £28,000

Income tax is payable on your total income after deducting your personal allowances and allowable expenses.

   †The 20% rate instead of basic rate applies to savings income above the starting band but within the basic rate band, excluding dividends.

Capital gains tax
The rate for individuals is the same as their income tax rate.

	2001–2002	2000–2001	1999–2000
Exemption limit	£7,500	£7,200	£7,100

Inheritance tax
Rate 40%

	2001–2002	2000–2001	1999–2000
Exemption limit	£242,000	£234,000	£231,000

VAT standard rate	17.5%	17.5%	17.5%
VAT registration turnover level	£54,000 from 1.4.2001	£52,000 from 1.4.2000	£51,000 from 1.4.99
VAT deregistration turnover level	£52,000 from 1.4.2001	£50,000 from 1.4.2000	£49,000 from 1.4.99

Corporation tax – The full rate for 1999–2000 through to 2001–2002 is 30% and 20% for small companies; for companies with trading profits up to £10,000 the rate is 10% from 1 April 2000 with marginal relief up to £50,000.

	2001–2002	2000–2001	1999–2000
Personal allowance	£4,535	£4,385	£4,335
Married Couple's allowance (Under 65)	Nil	Nil	††£1,970
Age allowance			
Aged 65–74 personal	£5,990	£5,790	£5,720
married couple's	††£5,365	††£5,185	††£5,125
Aged 75 & over personal	£6,260	£6,050	£5,980
married couple's	††£5,435	††£5,255	††£5,195
but there are income restrictions			
Income limit	£17,600	£17,000	£16,800
Additional personal allowance	Nil	Nil	††£1,970
Widow's bereavement allowance	Nil	Nil	††£1,970
Blind person's allowance	£1,450	£1,400	£1,380

††relief restricted to 10 per cent

Useful Inland Revenue contact numbers

If you want to order supplementary tax return sheets

telephone: 0845 9000 404
fax: 0845 9000 604

If you want to download the tax forms from the internet

www.inlandrevenue.gov.uk/sa
e-mail: saorderline.ir@gtnet.gov.uk

If you want to file your tax return electronically

www.ir-efile.gov.uk/
or telephone: 0845 605 5999

If you want general tax advice the helpline is

telephone: 0845 9000 444

If you are on low income and have had tax deducted from interest, etc. which you could claim back

telephone the taxback helpline: 0845 077 6543

If you are worried because you broke the tax rules and took out a maxi *and* a mini ISA in the same year

telephone the ISA helpline: 0845 604 1701

If you want details or help with claiming the children's tax credit

telephone: 0845 072 2020

If you want advice concerning National Insurance Contributions because you are a married woman paying reduced rate

telephone: 0845 915 5996

If you are newly self-employed

telephone: 0845 915 4515 or
0845 766 0830 in the Welsh language

If you want to claim the working families' tax credit or child care tax credit

telephone: 0800 597 5976

If you want to claim the disabled person's tax credit

telephone: 0845 605 5858

The following Inland Revenue booklets are also available from tax offices or on the internet on www.open.gov.uk/inrev/irleaf.htm

IR34	Pay As You Earn	FS1(MCA)	Married couple's allowance restriction
IR90	Tax allowances and reliefs	FS1(CTC)	Children's tax credit restriction
IR110	A guide for people with savings	CTCR1	Children's tax credit – Tax relief for families with children
IR120	You and the Inland Revenue		
IR121	Income tax and pensioners	WFTC/BK1	Your guide to working families' tax credit
IR170	Blind person's allowance	DPTC/BK1	Your guide to disabled person's tax credit
IR171	Income tax: a guide for people with children	WFTC/FS1	Factsheet – Working families' tax credit
IR172	Income tax and company cars	DPTC/FS1	Factsheet – Disabled person's tax credit
IR136	Income tax and company vans – A guide for employees and employers		

Significant dates for your diary

SIGNIFICANT DATES

2001 TAX RETURN

31 JANUARY 2001
Make first payment on account if applicable (see page 29).

APRIL 2001
You should receive a 2001 tax return.

APRIL/MAY 2001
Request any supplementary pages from tax office (ring 0845 9000 404 or fax 0845 9000 604).

31 JULY 2001
Make second payment on account if applicable.

30 SEPTEMBER 2001
Send in completed tax return.

31 JANUARY 2002
Send in tax return if you want to calculate your own tax. Pay any 2000–2001 balance.

2002 TAX RETURN

31 JANUARY 2002
Make first payment on account if applicable (see page 29).

APRIL 2002
You should receive a 2002 tax return.

APRIL/MAY 2002
Request any supplementary pages from tax office (ring 0845 9000 404 or fax 0845 9000 604).

31 JULY 2002
Make second payment on account if applicable.

30 SEPTEMBER 2002
Send in completed tax return.

31 JANUARY 2003
Send in tax return if you want to calculate your own tax. Pay any 2001–2002 balance.

30th September

31st January

Your tax organiser

When you fill in the self assessment tax return, you only have to put *total* figures in the various boxes. Use the following work sheets to record your figures.

Use the left-hand columns in the following work sheets to keep a record of how you arrived at these figures, not only as a convenient means of adding them up but also in case the tax office asks for the details.

Use the right-hand columns in the following work sheets to keep an ongoing record throughout this next year as a reminder of significant figures or events during 2001–2002 so that when you get next year's tax return to complete you have the information at your fingertips.

What you entered in your 2000–2001 tax return

Reminders to help you fill in your 2001–2002 tax return

INCOME FROM INTEREST AND SAVINGS

Paperwork to keep: interest statements; dividend vouchers; National Savings Certificates

Interest received and tax deducted

Are your investments in joint names? – see page 9

National Savings

Interest received and tax deducted

Are your investments in joint names? – see page 9

National Savings

What you entered in your 2000–2001 tax return

Reminders to help you fill in your 2001–2002 tax return

INCOME FROM DIVIDENDS

Paperwork to keep: dividend vouchers; contract notes

Dividends and tax deducted

Dividends and tax deducted

OTHER INCOME

Paperwork to keep: receipts and statements for casual earnings and expenses claimed

Other income

Other income

Expenses claimed

Expenses to be claimed

Remember to claim expenses – see page 34

Remember to claim expenses – see page 34

**What you entered in your
2000–2001 tax return**

**Reminders to help you fill in your
2001–2002 tax return**

INCOME FROM UK PENSIONS, RETIREMENT ANNUITIES AND SOCIAL SECURITY BENEFITS

Paperwork to keep: State pension book or details; P60 form for other pensions; DSS statements

State pension details

State pension details

**Other pensions and annuities
and tax deducted**

**Other pensions and annuities
and tax deducted**

Social security benefits

Social security benefits

What you entered in your 2000–2001 tax return	Reminders to help you fill in your 2001–2002 tax return

PAYMENTS ALLOWED FOR TAX

Paperwork to keep: pension statements; interest certificates; covenants; Gift Aid receipts; receipts for expenses, etc

Payments to pension schemes, etc.

Top up your pension contributions before the tax year ends – see page 16

Payments to pension schemes, etc.

Top up your pension contributions before the tax year ends – see page 16

Expenses claimed (subscriptions, loan interest, maintenance, etc.)

Expenses claimed (subscriptions, loan interest, maintenance, etc.)

Charitable giving (covenants, Gift Aid, etc.)

Charitable giving (covenants, Gift Aid, etc.)

What you entered in your 2000–2001 tax return	**Reminders to help you fill in your 2001–2002 tax return**

EMPLOYMENT

Paperwork to keep: P60, P45 & P11D forms; receipts for benefits; invoices for expenses, etc.

Diary note		**Diary note**	
P60 due from employer by	31 MAY 2001	P60 due from employer by	31 MAY 2002
P11D due from employer by	6 JULY 2001	P11D due from employer by	6 JULY 2002
Check your PAYE code	FEB/MAR 2001	Check your PAYE code	FEB/MAR 2002

Changes in employment (dates, etc.)   **Changes in employment** (dates, etc.)

Car mileage log   **Car mileage log**

Getting close to 18,000 business miles near the year end? – see page 59

Getting close to 18,000 business miles near the year end? – see page 59

Car changes (details)   **Car changes** (details)

Benefits received from employer   **Benefits received from employer**

Expenses claimed   **Expenses to be claimed**

Check what's available – see page 34

Check what's available – see page 34

What you entered in your 2000–2001 tax return	Reminders to help you fill in your 2001–2002 tax return

INCOME FROM LAND AND PROPERTY

Paperwork to keep: records of rents received; records of expenses and bills for them

Rent-a-Room Scheme	Rent-a-Room Scheme

Rent income received	Rent income received

Expenses claimed	Expenses to be claimed
Check expenses on page 46	*Check expenses on page 46*

FOREIGN INCOME AND EXPENSES

Paperwork to keep: overseas dividend vouchers; details of pensions; foreign tax assessments, etc

Income and tax paid	Income and tax paid

Expenses claimed	Expenses to be claimed

What you entered in your 2000–2001 tax return

Reminders to help you fill in your 2001–2002 tax return

PERSONAL ALLOWANCES

Do you need to consider transferring unused allowances to your wife or husband? ❏

Do you need to consider transferring unused allowances to your wife or husband? ❏

_____

_____

_____

_____

_____

_____

_____

_____

_____

_____

SHARE OPTIONS

Paperwork to keep: share option certificates; correspondence from trustees; market valuations

Share options granted, exercised, etc.

Share options granted, exercised, etc.

_____

_____

_____

_____

_____

_____

_____

_____

_____

_____

INCOME FROM TRUSTS, SETTLEMENTS, ESTATES etc

Paperwork to keep: dividend and interest vouchers; form R185E; trust correspondence

Interest

_____

Interest

_____

Dividends

_____

Dividends

_____

Other notes

_____

Other notes

_____

| What you entered in your 2000–2001 tax return | Reminders to help you fill in your 2001–2002 tax return |

SELF EMPLOYMENT AND PARTNERSHIPS

Paperwork to keep: all account books, sales and purchase invoices

Diary check

VAT limit OK? ☐   NI Payments OK? ☐

Payment on account made _____

Accounts completed ☐

Other notes

Diary check

VAT limit OK? ☐   NI Payments OK? ☐

Payment on account scheduled _____

Accounts preparation ☐

Other notes

There will be interest charges if you are late with 'on account' payments – see page 29

There will be interest charges if you are late with 'on account' payments – see page 29

What you entered in your 2000–2001 tax return	Reminders to help you fill in your 2001–2002 tax return

CAPITAL GAINS

Paperwork to keep: contract notes for sale or purchase of shares; invoices and letters for sale or purchase of other assets; invoices for allowable expenses

Assets purchased	**Assets purchased**
Assets sold	**Assets sold**
Expenses claimed	**Expenses to be claimed**
Indexation/tapering relief note	**Indexation/tapering relief note**
Losses brought forward or carried forward	**Losses brought forward or carried forward**

Forget me not